THE GOOD, THE BAD, AND THE UGLY DETROIT TIGERS

HEART-POUNDING, JAW-DROPPING, AND GUT-WRENCHING MOMENTS FROM DETROIT TIGERS HISTORY

George Cantor

Library of Congress Cataloging-in-Publication Data

Cantor, George, 1941–
The good, the bad, and the ugly Detroit Tigers : heart-pounding, jaw-dropping, and gut-wrenching moments from detroit tigers history / by George Cantor.
p. cm.
Includes bibliographical references.
ISBN-13: 978-1-60078-052-3
ISBN-10: 1-60078-052-0
1. Detroit Tigers (Baseball team)—History. 2. Baseball—Michigan—Detroit—History. I. Title.

GV875.D6C34 2007
796.357'640977434—dc22

2007040331

This book is available in quantity at special discounts for your group or organization. For further information, contact:

Triumph Books
542 South Dearborn Street
Suite 750
Chicago, Illinois 60605
(312) 939-3330
Fax (312) 663-3557

Printed in U.S.A.
ISBN: 978-1-60078-052-3
Design by Patricia Frey
All photos courtesy of AP/Wide World Photos except where otherwise indicated.

To Jerry Broad, Tom DeLisle,
Mike Cantor, Tom Huth, Jeff Shillman,
and all the others who cheered and suffered
with me over our hometown team.

and our favorite fan
Ron Del Bello
7/2012

CONTENTS

FOREWORD

I know the name of this book is *The Good, the Bad, and the Ugly Detroit Tigers*, but to tell you the truth, I don't have any really bad memories of my days in the big leagues. For me it was *all* good. All the things I dreamed about as a young person growing up in Detroit came true when I started playing for the Tigers.

Well, maybe there is one ugly memory. My first year down at Tigertown in Lakeland, Florida, I learned that I couldn't stay with the white players. I couldn't even ride in a white-owned taxicab. I had to live with a black family and walk four miles each way to get to Tigertown. That's just the way things were in Lakeland back in the early 1960s.

But I learned a good lesson from that ugliness. I took something bad and made it a positive. I tried to do what I could as a major league ballplayer to help fight discrimination. I knew firsthand what racism was like, and fighting it gave me a goal in life aside from playing ball. That's what people should do whenever something ugly happens to them: figure out how to shape that ugliness into a way to effect positive change.

I also think it's good to know more about the history of the Detroit Tigers. Both the fans and the ballplayers of today can stand to learn a little bit more about the players who went before them. Some of the players do ask questions when I work with them. Brandon Inge, for one, is very interested in baseball history. But some of the others are not so inquisitive.

I have my dad to thank for telling me about the past. When I was growing up, I was always hearing his stories about Jackie Robinson and Larry Doby. I remember at Northwestern High School, where I was a catcher, my coach, Sam Bishop, let me wear a glove that belonged to big-league catcher Harry Chiti. I slipped it on, and it was a great moment in my young life.

We used to sneak into Tiger Stadium when I was a kid. We'd be playing catch around the entrance, and when a dumpster went by, we'd jump inside to get through the gates. One time they caught us in the visitors' clubhouse. Rip Collins used to run it, and he was a great guy. Instead of calling the police, he introduced us to Rocky Colavito. The Rock was with Cleveland then, and when he met us, he was just as nice as he could be. We didn't mean anything to him. He didn't have to do that. From that day on, he was my hero, and meeting him again when I joined the Tigers was my biggest thrill. He continued to help me even though he knew I was going to take his job. He was passing on the legacy, and I tried to do the same thing when my day was almost over and Steve Kemp was coming up.

When I look back on my years with the Tigers, it is kind of funny. I came up as a home-run hitter, and that's how people knew about Willie Horton. Hitting came easy to me, but I don't know how many times I was out there practicing throws. Mickey Stanley spent hours teaching me the right way to throw on a line. And now I'm remembered most for my defense.

When I meet people today, the first thing they want to talk about is that throw in the 1968 World Series, the one where Lou Brock was out at the plate. That play didn't happen by accident. Bill Freehan worked out signals for letting a throw go through. It was the preparation that made it work. That's the big thing young players have to learn. Everybody wants to win, but not everybody wants to prepare. That's the difference.

While we're on the subject of defense, I still hold the Detroit record for most putouts in a game for an outfielder. I had 11 in one game in 1972, and they took me out early, too. More good memories—that's what I see when I look back.

—Willie Horton

THE GOOD

FOUR UNFORGETTABLE HITS [1935, 1945, 1968, 1984]

The Tigers have won four world championships. Strangely enough, when you add up the four big hits that sealed those deals, they reveal a cycle. Not only a cycle, but a progressive cycle.

A single in 1935. A double in 1945. A triple in 1968. A home run in 1984.

Goose Goslin. Paul Richards. Jim Northrup. Kirk Gibson. They got the four hits to remember, and what they did will never be forgotten in Detroit.

Goose's Single: 1935

When Goslin walked to the plate in the ninth inning of Game 6, the Tigers had endured decades of World Series frustration. They had lost all four times they made it there. In fact, just three other big-league teams—the lowly St. Louis Browns, the horrible Philadelphia Phillies, and the slaphappy Brooklyn Dodgers—had failed to win a championship by 1935.

It had been particularly galling the previous year. Detroit had taken a 3–2 lead back to Navin Field against the Cardinals, only to lose the final two. Now they were up 3–2 again, this time against the Cubs, and the score was tied 3–3.

Bottom of the ninth. A restless stirring within the crowd. So many had waited so long for something to cheer about in this Depression year. The Cubs had come dangerously close to breaking

Manager Mickey Cochrane crosses home plate on Goose Goslin's single in the ninth inning of the World Series against the Cubs on July 7, 1935. Goslin's hit forever etched him into Detroit Tigers lore.

it open in the top half of the inning. Stan Hack led off with a triple. But Tommy Bridges, a man with a curveball for every occasion, managed to get the last three hitters in the Chicago batting order, and Hack stayed put.

Cubs manager Charlie Grimm allowed his pitcher, Larry French, to bat with one out. His staff was worn out, and Grimm had said before the game that he had no one to bring in after French. Bridges got him on a bouncer back to the mound, then retired Augie Galan, and the threat was over.

But there was a sense of urgency in the Detroit dugout. Their big slugger, Hank Greenberg, was down with an injury, and memories of the previous year were all too fresh. The Tigers needed to end it now.

Manager Mickey Cochrane started it off with a one-out single. Then Charlie Gehringer smashed a wicked drive down the first-base line. It looked like a sure double that could score Cochrane with the game-winning run. But first baseman Phil Cavarretta made a sensational stab for the ball and stepped on first for the out. Cochrane could only advance to second.

Now it was Goslin's turn. This was his fifth Series, the most of any Tiger. He was nine days short of his 35th birthday, nearing the end of a Hall of Fame career. He had been acquired from the financially strapped Washington Senators before the 1934 season, and while his average had tailed off to .292 that year, he had still knocked in 109 runs. There was one more on the pond to pick up.

"I said to the plate umpire, 'If they pitch that ball over the plate, you can take that monkey suit off,'" said Goose. "And sure enough, the first ball French threw in there...zoom. Lucky hit. That's all that it was. Just a looper into right field. But you've got to be lucky to get up to bat at just the right time.

"Oh, did those Tigers fans go wild. I'll never forget it. You know, I played for three teams in my 18 years in the majors and I was with the Tigers for just four of them. But the best baseball town I ever played in was Detroit."

Richards's Double: 1945

Some baseball historians call the 1945 Series the worst ever played, which isn't altogether fair. World War II had been over for two months when the Series began, and people were eager for the return of good times. Normal times. But 4-Fs still dotted the rosters of the Tigers and the Cubs. Even the return of Greenberg, a bona fide superstar, couldn't change the fans' perception that they were watching a bogus Series.

The feeling was heightened when Detroit's Chuck Hostetler fell down rounding third with what would have been the winning run in Game 6. Instead, the Cubs pulled it out in 12 innings and forced a seventh game, to be played at Wrigley Field.

Just as in 1935, though, their manager, Grimm, had an exhausted pitching staff. His most effective starter was Hank

Borowy. He had shut out the Tigers in Game 1 and then threw four innings of relief to stop them again in Game 6.

In an incredible gamble, Grimm decided to start Borowy again on one day's rest in the deciding game. Moreover, his opponent was Hal Newhouser, a 25-game winner and the American League MVP for the second straight year.

The Cubs had hammered Newhouser in Game 1, though, and hit him pretty well in a Game 5 loss. Grimm felt they could get to him again if Borowy just held off the Tigers for a while.

But Borowy's tank was empty. Three straight singles drove him from the game in the first inning and brought on Paul Derringer. He had beaten the Tigers in Game 7 in Cincinnati in 1940 and he got two quick outs now, but then forced in another run with a walk. Now it was 2–0. Next to the plate was Paul Richards, a weak-hitting catcher who had gone just two-for-15 in the Series. If they could get him out, the inning would be over—and the Cubs would still have a chance.

Richards may have been the paradigmatic wartime ballplayer. He was almost 37 years old and had spent seven straight years in the minors before the Tigers bought his contract in 1943. The intention was to make him Newhouser's valet.

Newhouser had been a big disappointment. A starter as an 18-year-old rookie, he had seemed to be regressing every year since. Tigers management was convinced the problems were in his head, and that a wise old soul like Richards behind the plate could straighten him out.

The plan worked to perfection. By 1945 Newhouser was the best pitcher in baseball, and Richards replaced regular catcher Bob Swift every time Newhouser started. A career .227 hitter, Richards now found himself at the plate at the most critical moment of the Series.

His future teammate, George Kell, said of Richards, "He wakes up every morning, looks in the mirror, and says, 'I'm Paul Richards and I'm tough.'" It was that attitude that came to the fore now. He drove Derringer's offering into the left-field corner for a three-run double. The Tigers had handed Newhouser a five-run lead and that was more than enough as Detroit cruised home, 9–3.

Richards played one more season in Detroit before embarking on a career with the White Sox and the Orioles that established his reputation as the most cerebral manager of his time. But he never again made it to the Series.

Northrup's Triple: 1968

By the seventh inning, the tension at Busch Stadium was unbearable. This was supposed to be a St. Louis walkover. Even after the Tigers had come back from a 3–1 deficit to force a seventh game, they still had to get past Bob Gibson to win it. And he, quite simply, was unbeatable.

He had been the hero of the Cards' Series wins in 1964 and 1967 and had handled the Tigers easily in two previous starts this time around. But now he was hooked up in a 0–0 duel with Mickey Lolich, and as the innings passed, Lolich seemed to be getting stronger.

Lolich had pulled out of big trouble by picking off two of the best St. Louis base runners, Lou Brock and Curt Flood, in the sixth. But Detroit couldn't muster anything even resembling a threat and had a total of only one hit going into the seventh.

When Norm Cash singled with two outs, it seemed harmless enough. Then Willie Horton grounded a single through the left side. Now it was Jim Northrup's turn.

The slender outfielder, in his third season as a starter, had been a top prospect in the Tigers farm system after an outstanding athletic career at Alma College in Michigan. This had been his most productive year, with 90 RBIs. Sixteen of them had come on just four swings of the bat.

Northrup had launched four grand-slam homers, including two in one game, and then added a fifth in Game 6 of the Series. Veteran play-by-play announcer Ernie Harwell had taken to referring to him as "the Slammer Himself."

Gibson went right after him, anxious to snuff out this little threat quickly and get his team back at bat. Northrup's response was a dart to dead center, where Flood, one of the best defensive outfielders in the game, waited. But he took one step in, and when he tried to pivot back, his footing slipped on turf sloppy from rain and a recent football game. The ball landed behind him, Northrup raced to third, the Tigers had a 2–0 lead, and with it the Series.

"Even if he broke back right away, no way does he catch that ball," Northrup always insisted.

Horton expressed it even better, saying, "I touched the plate, looked up, and I saw Rudolph the Red-Nosed Reindeer coming over the left-field roof."

The Tigers had their biggest Series upset ever.

Gibson's Homer: 1984

The news photograph hung in Michigan homes for years. Here was Kirk Gibson, uniform pants filthy and torn, arms upraised in a bellow of triumph, returning to the dugout after his three-run homer put away San Diego for keeps.

The Padres were huge underdogs in this Series, but they were pesky. Their starters couldn't get past the third inning in four of the five games, their slugging left fielder Kevin McReynolds was injured. But still they kept hanging around.

The Tigers were up three games to one, but if they lost this one, the Series would return to California, and the Padres had whipped the Cubs three-straight there in the playoffs. So there was a strong sense that it must be finished now.

GIANT KILLER

One of the best Tigers comeback players was Harry Coveleski. He was called the Giant Killer because in his rookie year with the Phillies, 1908, he beat New York three times in the stretch and kept them from winning the pennant. But he could not regain that form in subsequent seasons, and arm problems sent him to the minors for six years.

He resurfaced with Detroit in 1914 and then won 65 games over the next three seasons. He nearly pitched the team to a pennant in 1915. Coveleski's rebound was brief, though. At the age of 31, his arm problems returned, and within two years he was out of baseball. But it was great while it lasted.

OVERLOOKED STAR

The most underrated Tigers hitter of all time probably is Bobby Veach. In 12 seasons, he averaged .312 in hitting, drove in more than 100 runs six times, and played a strong left field.

During his entire career in Detroit, from 1912 to 1923, the other outfielders in the lineup were Ty Cobb, Sam Crawford, and Harry Heilmann. Three Hall of Famers. It was pretty easy to be overlooked in that group. So Veach remains the forgotten man, almost never mentioned among great Detroit outfielders of the past.

Game 5 fit the pattern. Mark Thurmond was routed in the first inning, but Detroit lost a 3–0 lead. As the Tigers came to bat in the eighth, they were clinging to a 5–4 advantage.

On the mound was an old nemesis, Goose Gossage, who had toyed with the Tigers when he was the top reliever with the Yankees. He had lost a little off his fastball at age 33, but it was still good enough to close for the National League champs.

The first two hitters reached base in the eighth and were sacrificed to second and third. That brought Gibson to bat, with Lance Parrish on deck. The obvious play was an intentional pass, hoping Parrish would then hit something on the ground. That's what manager Dick Williams called, but to his astonishment Gossage waved him off. Williams trotted out to the mound to make sure he and Gossage understood each other.

Gibson watched and prepared himself.

"He [Gossage] had just abused me in the past," said Gibson. "I knew what he was thinking. What he didn't realize, though, was that he had just given me the challenge I needed."

Gibson was a superstar athlete, an All-American receiver at Michigan State who could have been an NFL standout. Instead, he chose baseball and was touted as a player "who had a chance to be the next Mickey Mantle."

But it wasn't happening, and in 1983 his performance had been so bad (a .227 average and just 15 homers) that he went to

Seattle after the season to clear his head. He came back as a force, the team's top run-producer and its emotional leader. Now the promise had met the moment.

Gossage's second pitch was sent on a line into the right-field upper deck. The Tigers' lead was now 8–4, and everyone knew it was over. The ninth was only a formality.

It was the last Series game ever played at Michigan and Trumbull and gave the old ballpark one of its most indelible memories.

MAGGLIO THE MAGNIFICENT (2006)

It was an incredible capper to an impossible year. The Tigers jumped and howled at the plate in Comerica Park as Magglio Ordonez circled the bases on a chilly October night, running toward home.

The doormats of the American League had won the playoffs and were going to the World Series. Had anyone at that ballpark said he knew that was going to happen when the 2006 season began, you'd have strapped him up and taken out the polygraph. Delirious doesn't even begin to describe the feeling.

It was richly symbolic that the three-run homer that finished the playoff sweep of Oakland was hit by Ordonez. After exploring new depths of awfulness in 2003, the Tigers had picked up three high-profile free agents in the long struggle back to respectability.

First there was catcher Pudge Rodriguez. This year it had been left-handed starter Kenny Rogers. In between was Ordonez, cut loose by the White Sox after a debilitating leg injury. He had been one of the top sluggers in the league for several seasons, but Chicago figured he was past his prime. Then the Sox turned around and won the World Series without him in 2005.

"That was the most painful experience I ever had, watching that on TV," he said afterward. "I made up my mind that I had to use it as motivation."

Ordonez was still hampered by his injury in his first year in Detroit. The power stroke wasn't there. But in 2006 he held down the cleanup spot, and while it was apparent that he wasn't entirely back to normal, it was still good enough for 104 RBIs and 24 homers.

Rogers had already paid off big, winning 17 games during the season, stabilizing the pitching staff, and shutting out the Yankees and Oakland in his playoff starts. The game with New York, before the loudest, most jubilant crowd in Comerica history, set the tone for the postseason celebration.

The Tigers took care of the A's twice in Oakland and went up 3–0 once the Series returned to Detroit. But there was still one to go, and the Yankees had demonstrated in 2004 how very wrong things could turn for a team with that lead.

Oakland went ahead 3–0 in this game, and even when the Tigers came back to tie it, there was still room for painful doubt. So much had gone wrong in the recent past. No one could be sure until the coffin lid slammed down hard on the A's.

Magglio Ordonez added to a memorable season when he hit a three-run homer against the Oakland A's to win Game 4 of the ALCS. The Tigers defeated the A's 6–3 to win the series. Photo courtesy of Getty Images.

The first two Tigers went down in the ninth. Then Craig Monroe and Placido Polanco laced out singles against reliever Huston Street. Ordonez's ensuing blast went deep into the left-field seats, gone from the get-go. As radio announcer Dan Dickerson hollered, "The Tigers are going to the World Series!" the city erupted in an outburst of joyful disbelief.

Even their subsequent five-game loss to the Cards in the World Series couldn't dampen the sheer exhilaration of that moment.

WHAM! HERE I AM (1965, 1976)

Two of the most explosive arrivals to the Tigers were Willie Horton and Mark Fidrych. When they made their opening statements, there was little doubt that Detroit fans were seeing the introductions of two stars.

Horton came first in 1965. The entire city had been waiting for him. He was one of the biggest signings of the decade, a star on the Detroit sandlots. He had made appearances in 40 games with the team the previous two years, just enough to tease everyone with the potential of what could be.

Although he hit just .220 with two homers in these brief trials, it was enough for the Tigers to clear the way by trading left fielder Rocky Colavito. That saddened Horton.

"My first time up with the team I went up to Rock and told him how much I admired him when I was growing up," said Horton. "He thanked me and said that he was going to be traded because of me. He wasn't mad or anything, it was just the way things were. Still, it gave you a funny feeling."

Horton was given the starting job in 1965 and suffered through a lackluster April. But then the calendar turned, and what happened next has gone down in Tigers lore as the "Seven Games in May."

Between the 11th and 18th of that month, Horton utterly destroyed the Washington and Boston pitching staffs. He went off on a tear that included six home runs, 18 RBIs, a batting average of .588, and a slugging percentage of 1.235.

The outburst launched the Tigers on a run that had them in the pennant race until August. Just as important, it gave a preview of things to come. Horton finished the season with 29 homers and 104 RBIs and was installed as Detroit's cleanup man for the next 11 years.

Move the calendar ahead to May 1976. Horton was now 33 years old and in his last full season with the team. Then along came Fidrych.

It was obvious this team wasn't going anywhere. The veterans who had won a championship in 1968 and a division title in 1972 were either gone or going. The Tigers had lost 102 games the previous year and weren't supposed to do much better this time around.

On May 15, a 21-year-old, gangly, frizzy-haired right-hander was called up from the minors. He was handed the ball to start against Cleveland, and when the ball was placed in his hand, he talked to it. He got on his hands and knees and landscaped the mound. He went over and bucked up his teammates if they made an error. He looked like Big Bird on *Sesame Street*. So the legend of "Mark the Bird" was born.

The likable and quirky Mark Fidrych charmed fans upon his arrival in 1976 and put together one brilliant season.
Photo courtesy of Getty Images.

He beat the Indians on a two-hitter that day, 2–1, before a tiny Saturday afternoon crowd. He didn't win his second until two weeks later when he went all 11 innings to beat Milwaukee. Then he did the same thing at Texas.

Now the crowds were starting to build. Not only was Fidrych pitching strong, complete games, but the team seemed inspired, winning behind him with last-ditch rallies in the ninth or in extra innings.

By the time the Yankees came to town in late June for a nationally televised Monday night game, the Bird was 7–1, and Detroit was in a frenzy. With a crowd of 48,000 on its feet and yelling "Go, Bird, Go," Fidrych stifled the Yankees (who would win the pennant that year) 5–1. He was now a true American idol.

Cakes arrived in the clubhouse with the phone numbers of lady admirers attached. He was mobbed by autograph seekers on the streets. The man who had arrived almost anonymously in Detroit just six weeks before was now the prince of the city.

Still it went on. A full house of 51,000 came out to watch Fidrych blank Baltimore, and then they packed the stadium again a few days later against Kansas City. He went 11 innings once more and shut out Oakland 1–0. He started the All-Star Game. When he beat Minnesota on July 20, he was 11–2. Twins owner Calvin Griffith marveled, "This young man is the hope of baseball."

But the hope faded. No one would have wanted to know it right then, but for the rest of his career Fidrych would go just 18–17.

After being named Rookie of the Year, he hurt his leg the following year in spring training. As so often happens, the injury affected his delivery. He developed arm injuries that he could never quite overcome. By 1980, it was over.

But for one shining season, no one in Tigers history ever flew higher or landed more spectacularly than the Bird.

THAT'S *MISTER* BOBO TO YOU (1940)

Even before the biggest games there is always noise in a clubhouse. Punch lines to old jokes yelled across the room. Bats pounded against lockers. Insults cheerfully exchanged. Anything to work off the tension.

But on that day in 1940 it was dead quiet. An uneasy shuffling, almost apologetic in its muffled sound.

The big man in the far corner, old Buck Newsom, ordinarily would have been right in the middle of the fun, telling anyone who would listen how he was going to go out there and tie this Bobo up in knots with the hard curve and then blow him away with the pitch up and in.

But he sat red-eyed and alone. Other members of the Tigers would steal a look at him from time to time, trying to see how he was bearing up, whether he would be ready to go.

Fifth game of the 1940 World Series. Tied two games apiece with Cincinnati. They don't come much bigger than that.

Without Newsom, Detroit wouldn't even have been there. He had been called a braggart and a clown, and that was a pretty accurate description. He was also called baseball's Marco Polo because he played for 17 different teams in the majors and minors—including five trips to the Washington Senators alone.

Newsom was the only pitcher in modern baseball history to win more than 200 games and lose more than 200 games, too.

And for this one year he was also a helluva pitcher, the pitcher he always claimed to be. At 21–5, he had hit his stride. And there's no telling how many he would have won if he hadn't broken his thumb in July and been out for almost a month.

His whole family, proud as could be, took the train up from Hartsville, South Carolina, to watch him pitch the Series opener. It seemed like half the town was in Cinci for the game—the mayor, the boys who knew him when he pitched semipro ball for the Coker Mill team.

They'd always expected great things from him. No one could throw the ball like old Buck. It just took him a while to get there. But now here he was—33 years old (although he sometimes claimed to be 31)—and Newsom was going to make them all proud.

"He was just overpowering that season," recalled Hank Greenberg in later years. "He threw what they would later call a slider, and the hitters never quite caught up to it. He even got Joe DiMaggio out with it a few times, although Joe hit him about as well as anyone in the league. Better than I ever did when he was pitching with other teams. He'd keep it low on the outside corner, and I couldn't do anything with it."

"Everyone was 'Bobo' to him," said Hal Newhouser, another future Hall of Famer who was then in his rookie season. "He couldn't keep anyone's name straight. It was 'Bobo' whether you were Greenberg or just a punk kid like me. And so we all just called him 'Bobo' right back."

Even Ted Williams said that Newsom was one of the toughest pitchers he ever hit against. "That fastball would come out of a whirlwind of arms and legs, and you just couldn't pick it up until it was right at the plate," he said.

Until this season, though, no one had taken him seriously. Sure, he'd won 20 games for the St. Louis Browns in 1938, which was a bit difficult, seeing as how the entire team won just 55 times all year.

But he was a bigmouth, fighting with managers and umpires, refusing to hide behind a shield of false modesty, daring the world to discover his greatness.

"One Bobo told me that if I kept my mouth shut a little more and stopped being a clown, I could be a much better pitcher," he said. "I knew this Bobo won about twice as many games as me the last season, so I asked him what his salary was. It was a lot less than mine. So I told him, 'Who's the clown now?' He didn't have nothin' to say after that."

Now Bobo was laughing at them all.

His dad, Henry, had seen him in the big leagues just once before. But on October 2, he was in the stands at Crosley Field to watch his son pitch the Series opener. Buck didn't let him down. He wasn't at his sharpest, but the Tigers drove Reds starter Paul Derringer from the mound in the second inning and coasted to a 7–2 victory. Newsom went all the way and gave up only eight hits.

The party started right after the ninth inning. Buck was intent on showing his family and friends all the wonders of Cincinnati, and the celebration went on for hours.

Henry Newsom went back to his room at the Gibson Hotel, and in the middle of the night, following the happiest day of his life, he died of a heart attack.

While his team was losing to the Reds the next day, a tearful Buck Newsom rode the train back to Hartsville with the family and friends who had come in jubilation and returned in mourning.

There were no days off scheduled for this Series, and Buck wasn't supposed to pitch again until Game 5, back in Detroit. Manager Del Baker had gone to him and told Buck that everyone would understand if he decided to stay at home with his family. Newsom shook his head and swore that he'd be back in Detroit when he was needed.

And there he was, getting himself ready for the biggest game of his life. A story developed over time that Newsom stood in the clubhouse before this game and threatened to fight anyone who lost it for him. But sportswriters of that era tended to embellish such tales or make them up entirely if no better angle was at hand.

It was also a highly unlikely scenario. This was a veteran team that didn't need any prompting to recall what was at stake.

Greenberg was at his peak, finishing up a Most Valuable Player season. He had led the league in homers and runs batted in and hit a career-best .340. Most important, he also had agreed to move to left field to make room for Rudy York at first base.

The Tigers had struggled valiantly to make York into a catcher or third baseman. But by now it was apparent that wasn't going to work. He could do far less damage defensively at first base, but only if Greenberg, the established star, agreed to the shift. He did, and York rewarded his sacrifice, finishing second to him in RBIs.

There was Charlie Gehringer, near the end of his long career but still a .300 hitter and a brilliant fielder. The fourth Hall of Fame player on this team, along with Newhouser, was Earl Averill. A top slugger with Cleveland throughout the '30s, he was now a deadly pinch-hitter as his career wound down.

This was a tough, experienced team, although no one expected them to win the pennant. They finished 26½ games behind the

Yankees in 1939, and then they had to beat the great Bob Feller on the final weekend of the season to get into the Series.

But they all knew what their top pitcher was going through. Nothing more needed to be said as the Tigers started to walk down the tunnel to the Briggs Stadium playing field while Bobo prepared for the game of his life.

The Reds never had a chance. Newsom stoned them 8–0 on a three-hitter. Two days later he had them stopped again in the seventh inning of Game 7, 1–0, when fielding miscues cost the Tigers the game and the Series. Just two innings more and Bobo would have joined Mickey Lolich at the summit of Tigers pitching history with three Series wins.

Bobo was never the same after that, although he stayed in the majors another 13 years. But for a few shining moments, Newsom—the clown and braggart—was the best there was.

LOLICH TIME [1968]

By his own admission, Mickey Lolich did not quite fit the heroic mold. He was just a stocky, blue-collar guy from Oregon who loved to ride motorcycles. They may have called him a typically wacky left-hander, but he insisted that wasn't true either. Well, maybe the wacky part, but he was a natural right-hander. He had to switch, he insisted, when a chopper fell on his right shoulder.

Lolich hadn't even been rated a top prospect coming through the farm system. He was wild and sometimes lost focus. But when they shipped him out to play for one season in his hometown of Portland, something seemed to click.

"The fences were so short there you couldn't make a mistake," he said. "I had to concentrate on every pitch. It changed my approach to pitching."

With that turnaround, he made it to the Tigers in 1963 and one year later won 18 games. Still, he seemed destined to play permanent second fiddle; never the leading man but sometimes the sidekick.

With the arrival of the one-man circus known as Denny McLain, Lolich faded from the spotlight. He became the number two, or sometimes number-three, guy on the staff. There were many times when he seemed unsure of himself, lacking confidence in his pitching ability.

When he was on, he could be extraordinary, and he nearly pitched the Tigers into a pennant with a late surge in 1967. But with the new season, as the team broke away from the rest of the league, Lolich was losing about as often as he was winning through the middle of summer.

Still, when the Cardinals went over the scouting reports on the Tigers, veteran American Leaguer Roger Maris warned his teammates that they probably could handle McLain, but look out for Lolich.

Another late-season rally brought him to a 17–9 record, his second best in the majors. But when the Series began, it was all about McLain and Bob Gibson, ballyhooed as a pitching matchup for the ages.

All Tigers fans remember what Lolich did with his arm in this Series. But what he did with his bat isn't recalled nearly as well as it should be. His win in Game 2 featured the only home run he ever hit in the bigs. He was so unaccustomed to circling the bases that he missed first on his first pass at it and had to come back a few steps to touch it.

When he started again, it was desperation time. The Tigers were down three games to one and facing extinction. Orlando Cepeda cracked a three-run homer off him in the first inning, and it certainly appeared to be the long good-bye.

But the team battled back and, incredibly, with Detroit still trailing 3–2 in the seventh, Lolich, a career .110 hitter, was allowed to bat for himself. Even more incredibly, he singled and started the rally that won the game. He did it all in Game 5.

Three days later he had to go out and do it all over again, matched against Gibson in Busch Stadium. In later years Lolich swore that he had no nerves at all on a day when the entire state of Michigan carried a rock of dread in its gut.

"I was worried about getting my relatives back to Detroit after the game because the Tigers wouldn't let them on the team plane and there were no tickets available anywhere else," he said many years later. "I spent so much time getting that straightened out that I didn't have a chance to eat and about halfway through the game I was starving. People wondered what [catcher Bill] Freehan and I were talking about late in the game. That was it. But nervous? Not really."

The 4–1 masterpiece he fashioned to win his third game of the Series, and the 16 straight shutout innings he threw to stave off the Cardinals with everything at stake, were for many Tigers fans the greatest sports experiences of their lives.

Maybe he didn't look much like a hero. But Lolich is just fine until the "real thing" comes along.

BREAKING THE BARRIER (1958)

It had been 11 long years, and the black fans in Detroit were sick of excuses. Jackie Robinson broke Major League Baseball's color line in 1947; the Tigers and the Red Sox remained the last two teams never to field a black player as the 1958 season began.

Many of the fans in Detroit switched their allegiance to Cleveland or the White Sox, two teams that had developed outstanding African American players. When the Indians came to town with a lineup that featured Larry Doby, Luke Easter, and perhaps an appearance by Satchel Paige, there was little doubt which side most black fans in the stands were pulling for.

Cleveland and the Sox also turned into perennial contenders through the 1950s, while the Tigers always settled in at the middle of the pack. In the minds of many fans, it was the failure to sign black players that was largely responsible.

Even the lordly Yankees, who had also refrained from fielding any black athletes, brought up Elston Howard in 1955. He was now established as a regular on four pennant winners.

Detroit's Negro League franchise had been well supported. One of its stars, Turkey Stearnes, even ended up in Cooperstown. Black community leaders couldn't understand why the Tigers didn't take advantage of this fan base and expressed their concerns to team officials. They were assured that the Tigers were looking for the right player.

But that player was certainly proving hard to find. Detroit had signed a few black players to minor league contracts. Infielders Jake Wood and George Smith were in their farm system. But none had yet worn a Tigers uniform, and it was becoming an embarrassing issue.

After the 1957 season, the Tigers cut a deal with the New York Giants. They obtained a part-time first baseman, Gail Harris, who sometimes hit for power, and a black infielder, Ozzie Virgil. The Giants were among the first teams to sign African Americans. Among them was the best player in the game, Willie Mays. But in his one season in New York, Virgil already had set another landmark. He became the first player born in the Dominican Republic to play in the majors.

In another few years this Caribbean nation would begin to send a steady stream of baseball talent to the majors. But Virgil was the pioneer, and he was about to break a second barrier in Detroit.

When the 1958 season began, Harris came north from spring training with the big club and Virgil remained in the minors. After two months it was clear that this was to be another nowhere year for the Tigers. The production of third baseman Reno Bertoia, who had shown some promise the previous season, tailed off considerably. On June 6 Virgil got the call and joined the team.

Everyone in the organization, of course, knew the significance of this move. So it was decided to take as much pressure as possible off Virgil and place him in the lineup for the first time at the start of an 11-game road trip. His debut as a Tiger came before 6,300 rather uninterested spectators in Washington. Virgil played third, batted sixth, and went one-for-five with a double in an 11–2 Detroit romp.

It wasn't until June 17 that he walked onto the field at Briggs Stadium for the first time. It was a Tuesday night game with the Senators, two teams that were going no place in particular. Yet nearly 30,000 fans showed up to watch. And a bit of history was made.

Virgil did not disappoint them. In an unforgettable Detroit debut, he went a perfect five-for-five. He doubled his first time up

LOCAL BOYS MAKE GOOD

There was a time in major league history when baseball teams were filled with local heroes. But the draft ended all that and it is a rarity, except among the California teams, to have players who grew up in the area playing for the same team they cheered for as children.

An exception was the 1968 Tigers. This was a throwback team, with no fewer than four key players having Michigan ties. Willie Horton and Bill Freehan were both sandlot stars in Detroit, although Freehan went to high school in Florida. Jim Northrup came from the tiny town of Breckenridge in the center of the state and Mickey Stanley was out of Grand Rapids.

Other local stars who made good in Motown were Hal Newhouser, Ted Gray, and Ray Herbert from Detroit; Charlie Gehringer from Fowlerville; Kirk Gibson from Waterford; Charlie Maxwell from Lawton; and Phil Regan and Dave Rozema from the western part of the state.

and then started a seven-run rally in the third with a leadoff single. It was everything the Tigers could have hoped for. Everyone had to be happy.

But the black community was not buying it. In their minds, the Tigers had come in through the back door.

"I was never accepted by the black fans in Detroit," Virgil recalled many years later. "They always thought of me as an outsider from the islands, not someone who was really part of the black community in America."

The issue wouldn't be resolved until the Tigers traded for Larry Doby and placed him in left field for the 1959 season. Unfortunately, Doby, who admitted to being 35 but was probably older, was nearing the end of his great career. He played just 18 games before being traded. It wasn't until Wood and Billy Bruton reached the Tigers in tandem in 1961 that a black presence was established on the team.

Virgil, naturally, could not maintain his sizzling start and finished the year hitting just .244. The Tigers traded for Eddie Yost to play third, and Virgil spent all of the next season in the minors. He came back as a utility man in 1960 and then was traded to Kansas City.

His entire stat line in the majors consists of only 324 games. But after all, breaking two barriers in one career is a fairly decent accomplishment.

THE BAD

WHAT A CATASTROPHE [2003]

The Tigers had gone through many disappointing seasons before. They sometimes fell well short of expectations. Five times they even lost more than 100 games.

But nothing even came close to the utter disaster of 2003. With 119 losses, they not only posted the worst record in franchise history, they came within one defeat of the all-time modern record, set by the 1962 Mets, a team so famously inept they led their manager Casey Stengel to exclaim, "Can't anybody here play this game?"

But the Mets were an expansion team at a time when people didn't understand how to assemble an expansion team, and there was no free agency to speed development. The Tigers of 2003 had no such excuses. They'd been given 102 years to screw things up.

In all fairness, this was a demolition by design. Team president Dave Dombrowski had been brought in to blow it up, end a decade and a half of mediocrity, and start all over again. He cleaned house, throwing out anyone who looked like a ballplayer, getting whatever he could for them in prospects and small change. Then he brought back Alan Trammell from San Diego, who had been minding his own business as a coach, to manage this mess.

Trammell had never managed at any level. But he was a bona fide hero, the star of the last championship Tigers team in 1984.

The Tigers didn't seem to know what direction they wanted to go during the disastrous 2003 season. Photo courtesy of Getty Images.

Dombrowski knew it was going to get ugly, and he hoped the return of Trammell would ease the agony for fans with any degree of loyalty.

But even Dombrowski couldn't have guessed how bad it was going to get. Losing the first nine games in a row and being outscored 14–54 may have given him a clue. But that was, literally, just for starters.

After winning once, they dropped eight more. By the end of April their record was 3–21, and even mediocrity was clearly beyond this team's reach.

Bad? The 2003 Tigers left bad behind before the buds burst out on the cherry trees. By mid-June, starter Mike Maroth was 1–11, and right beyond him was Jeremy Bonderman at 2–10. Serious discussion was given to holding these promising young pitchers out of the rotation for a while so as not to do permanent damage to their psyches.

Trammell had addressed criticism of his selection as manager before the season and dismissed it.

"It's true I've never managed before," he said. "But I learned from one of the best in Sparky Anderson. I believe I have a good instinctive feeling for what to do in most situations.

"I brought in Kirk Gibson and Lance Parrish as coaches, and both of these guys are proven winners. As for people who don't think I'm tough enough, all I can say is that they don't know me very well. Anyone who does knows that I can be a red ass when I have to be."

But instinct, attitude, and the color of one's derriere were not enough in a situation where there was simply no talent to put on the field.

By the end of July, the Tigers were already 50 games under .500. One losing streak blended into the next. In their fourth season at Comerica Park, the stadium that was supposed to rejuvenate the franchise and give it the funds to compete for talent, attendance dropped by almost 50 percent since its first year of operation. At 1.3 million, it was barely higher than the figures had been at Tiger Stadium in the mid-1990s, attendance figures that had prompted the drive for a new stadium.

But as the losses mounted and the once-proud franchise became a national joke on late-night television, something was stirring below the radar. Players like Brandon Inge, Craig Monroe, and Omar Infante, along with Maroth and Bonderman, were getting their trial by fire.

Far from wounding their self-esteem, the experience seemed to toughen them. Nothing they faced in the future would be as hard as going out to play day after day knowing they were going to get their tails whipped.

Maroth flatly refused to leave the rotation to avoid becoming the first pitcher in 23 years to lose 20 games. Trammell shunted aside all excuses. "We have to be held accountable," he said.

By September 12 the Tigers were 70 games under .500 and just 12 shy of the record for losses. Then they went into a slump.

With only 16 games left on the schedule, it had seemed likely that they would avoid the ultimate embarrassment. But 10 straight losses put them at 38–118. If anything in this nightmarish season could be called valiant, however, the Tigers somehow supplied it in their last six games. They won five of them and escaped the onus of being the worst team ever by the margin of one defeat.

Even that wasn't easy. Although their opponent in the final four-game series was Minnesota, which already had wrapped up the division title, the Twins declined to roll over. They forced the Tigers to 11 innings to win the first game and then put Detroit one game from the record by beating them in 11.

But it was the penultimate game of the season that salvaged some measure of respect. With the Twins regulars in the lineup and Brad Radke on the mound, Minnesota went off to an 8–0 lead. With that, the starters came out of the game. But the Tigers refused to go quietly down to infamy.

Storming back against the Twins bullpen, which included highly regarded Juan Rincon along with veterans J.C. Romero and Jessie Orosco, Detroit rallied for three in the seventh and four in the eighth to forge a tie.

Then in the ninth, Alex Sanchez walked, stole second and third, and scored on a wild pitch. The Tigers won 9–8, and from the mobbing of Sanchez at the plate, you'd have thought the pennant had just been clinched. Next day they won again, 9–4.

The Mets' record was safe, and the Tigers had extracted the tiniest sliver of sunshine from a season in the sewers.

ROBBY'S ROCK [1950]

There are errors that haunt a franchise forever. Some are physical, as with Bill Buckner's blunder with Boston in the 1986 World Series. Some are mental, as with the Giants' Fred Merkle's failure to touch second in a pennant-deciding game in 1908.

Detroit's contribution to this melancholy lore is the misplay by catcher Aaron Robinson in 1950. It has come down through time as "Robby's Rock." It was not the main reason the Tigers lost the pennant that year. Coming as it did, however, on the next-to-last weekend of the season, its importance was magnified many times over.

To compound the mistake, Robinson was the central figure in what is generally acknowledged as the worst trade Detroit ever made. To get him, they dealt young left-hander Billy Pierce to the White Sox after the 1948 season. Pierce then became one of the league's dominant pitchers for the next decade.

The trade did kind of make sense at the time. General Manager Billy Evans figured he was close to having a contending team, except for a catcher. He also had another promising young left-hander in Ted Gray to go along with veteran Hal Newhouser as a starter. Both Gray and Pierce were local boys, but Gray seemed a bit more advanced at the time. So Pierce was dealt, and, to add insult to injury, the Tigers also had to throw in some cash.

Robinson was even regarded as a good pickup. He had come up with the Yankees and looked as if he would settle in as their starting catcher after a strong season in 1946. But then a chap named Yogi Berra arrived from the minors, and Robby was out of a job.

The Yanks pulled off their own swindle in dealing him to Chicago. In return, they got junkballer Eddie Lopat, who was a prime-time starter on five of New York's championship teams. So there was a degree of rough justice in the fact that Chicago managed to end up with Pierce when they, in turn, decided to deal Robinson.

Robinson was a left-handed hitter, always desirable for Briggs Stadium's short right field, and he did hit 13 homers in 1949. When the Tigers got involved in a fierce four-team race the next year, though, his production dwindled away. Still, there was no one better around, and he kept the job by default.

Only six games would separate the league's top four teams at the end of the season. The Tigers wound up their schedule with two home-and-home series with the Indians, another of the contenders. For a time it appeared Detroit would take command of the race in midsummer. But the Yankees did what the Yankees always seemed to do. They pulled out a magic ticket and called up Whitey Ford from their farm system. He

FAREWELL, YANKEE KILLER

In the middle of the ballgame, a figure in street clothes walked onto the field at Tiger Stadium to wave good-bye. Frank Lary had just been traded and he was saying farewell to the fans in 1964.

It was a sad postscript to a heroic career for the Yankee Killer. He pitched the home opener in 1962 against the hated New Yorkers. It was a bitterly cold afternoon, with temperatures in the 30s and snow blowing in the air. The Tigers trailed 3–2 in the seventh when Lary came to bat. He drilled one into the right-center alley and raced to third for a game-tying triple. But on the way he pulled a hamstring and had to leave the game.

He had beaten the Yankees again. But Lary rushed his return from the injury, could not overcome his arm problems, and won just 10 more games in his career.

The Tigers thought a 17–1 beating in Boston was pretty bad. But the next day, June 18, 1953, the Red Sox blasted them with 17 runs in one inning on the way to a 23–3 win. It remains the worst inning in Tigers history.

It wasn't a completely lost week, though. The very next day they signed Al Kaline to his first major league contract.

went 9–1 down the stretch and gave New York what it needed to separate from the pack.

When the Tigers went into Cleveland, however, they still had a good shot. This was a heavy-hitting team, with George Kell, Vic Wertz, and Hoot Evers all driving in more than 100 runs. But Cleveland had three Hall of Famers in its starting rotation—Bob Feller, Bob Lemon, and Early Wynn.

Feller outdueled Newhouser in the first game and then the Indians blasted open the next one, 10–2. Now on a Sunday afternoon, Gray and Lemon were hooked up in a 1–1 tie into the tenth. The Tigers were just one and a half games behind New York, and if they could pull this one out, there was still a chance.

After all, Detroit had won the pennant once every five years since 1935. Surely that meant there had to be some karma on the Tigers' side.

When the Indians loaded the bases with one out, however, it appeared the end had come. But karma had an even more unkind finish in store.

A grounder was hit to Dick Kryhoski at first. He touched the bag and then rifled the ball to Robinson at home for the double play. Contemporary reports of the game indicate that it was a hazy day in Cleveland. Smoke from forest fires in Canada was being driven across Lake Erie by a strong north wind and visibility was reduced.

Still, all Robinson had to do was look 90 feet down the first-base line to see what had happened. Instead, he caught the ball and simply stepped on the plate. But there was no force-out on the play. When Kryhoski touched first, it meant Robinson had to tag the runner coming in from third for the third out.

Robinson simply stood there with his foot on the plate as the winning run slid in beneath him. Cleveland won 2–1 and swept the series while the Tigers fell two and a half games behind the Yankees. It was a gap they could not make up.

Meanwhile, the White Sox discovered that Pierce was tipping his curveball by sticking out his tongue. He won 12 games in 1950 and for the rest of the '50s was a top starter on a team that was always in contention.

The Tigers, by contrast, collapsed in 1951 and plunged all the way to last place for the first time in team history the following year. By then, Robinson was out of baseball.

DEATH OF THE MANAGERS [1966]

Charlie Dressen was the original "you hold 'em close and I'll think of something" manager. He was also a student of the Casey Stengel School of Rhetoric, in which you could spend half an hour talking to him and not have the slightest idea what he had said.

He liked to make chili in the clubhouse and took almost as much pride in that as he did in his managing—and he took enormous pride in his managing.

The Tigers had hired Dressen in 1963 to be a teacher, to turn the young talent flowing out of their farm system into big leaguers.

He never got to see the payoff on all that tutelage. Instead, he became part of a devastating cycle of events to hit the manager's office at Tiger Stadium in 1966.

Dressen was sidelined by a heart attack that finally killed him that year. He was replaced by Bob Swift, and within two months Swift was also gone, a victim of cancer. Bewildered and demoralized, the Tigers limped home under the direction of coach Frank Skaff.

They had been predicted to contend for the pennant. But they spent more time at funerals than at celebrations.

Dressen was deeply respected in the baseball community when he joined the Tigers. He had managed the Brooklyn Dodgers to two pennants in the early 1950s but could not make it past the Yankees in the World Series. When he asked for an extended contract after the second flag, he was fired.

He was never out of a job for long, but never caught another winner either. When he was fired by the dreadful Washington Senators in 1957, Cookie Lavagetto, the coach who was named to replace him, muttered, "This is sickening." Dressen corrected him: "No, this is baseball."

He understood what the game was about, and his program was showing distinct signs of progress after three years in Detroit. Denny McLain was emerging as a star, and Willie Horton, who had lost his parents in an automobile accident, looked at Dressen as a surrogate father. The veterans bought into his line, too, and Al Kaline cheerfully greeted him as "Cholly."

The Tigers had unexpectedly stayed in the 1965 race until August and ended up winning a respectable 89 games. It was Dressen's personal high since leaving Brooklyn and he looked forward to a season of success. But just one month into it, he was struck down by a coronary. Still, there was reason to believe he would be back in the dugout before the season ended.

The reins were handed to Swift, who had never managed in the majors before. He had been with the organization in one capacity or another for 22 years, sharing catching duties on the 1945 championship team and several seasons thereafter. As dour as Dressen was garrulous, Swift nonetheless knew the drill and had the team in second place in mid-July with a 48–35 record.

Coming back from a road trip, however, he complained of intense stomach pains and went in for a medical examination. The diagnosis was the worst possible.

The relationship between manager and players is delicate in the best of times. With this second change in two months, morale was in shreds. Skaff was a baseball lifer who had spent most of his career in the minor leagues and found a niche in Detroit as a coach. He was a very nice man who was just not equipped to be a big-league manager. But everyone knew it was just a stopgap until Dressen could return.

The Tigers went 5–12 after Skaff took over and lost ground they never could regain to the hard-charging Baltimore Orioles. In August, as the players boarded the team bus outside the Shoreham Hotel in Washington, they were given the news that Dressen had passed away early that morning. Horton wept openly.

It was obvious that it was now Skaff's job to run out the string until a permanent successor could be named during the off-season. The team managed to limp home in third place, 10 games from the lead.

McLain won 20 for the first time, and Horton had his second big season in a row. The young Tigers Dressen had nurtured were primed to be champions in just two more years. But others would get the glory.

Swift passed away a bit more than two months after Dressen's death. It was the final knell of a tragic season.

THREE DINKY SINGLES (1961)

The 1961 pennant race has come down in baseball history as the season of the home run. For most of the year, Roger Maris and Mickey Mantle were engaged in a historic race to break Babe Ruth's record, with Maris winning it. A TV movie, *61**, celebrated the duel.

The Yankees then went on to take the World Series and reign as champions again. What is generally forgotten outside of Detroit is that for most of that summer the Tigers were running right with the Yanks. Their own two sluggers, Norm Cash and Rocky Colavito, found the stands over 40 times apiece.

At the end, however, it was three dinky singles, barely finding their way through the infield, that did Detroit in. On a sweltering Friday evening in a packed Yankee Stadium, they turned the race around.

It had been 11 years since the Tigers were in a pennant race. But big changes came this year. For the first time, Detroit was starting two black players in its lineup: center fielder Billy Bruton had come over from the Braves and rookie Jake Wood was playing second base. They gave the Tigers an element of speed that had been lacking before, and when they got on base, excited crowds urged them to "go." Their combined total of 52 stolen bases may not sound like much. But when compared to the lead-footed Detroit teams of the recent past, it was astonishing.

Another rookie, third baseman Steve Boros, got off to a fast start, and new manager Bob Scheffing was keeping things calm and focused. They won eight of their first nine, and behind a great pitching staff, anchored by Frank Lary, Jim Bunning, and Don Mossi, the Tigers were in first place on July 4.

The rivalry with the Yankees had grown especially intense. During a May series in New York, Colavito had charged into the stands to protect his dad, who was being heckled by a group of fans. Lary won that game with a ninth-inning homer. But Lary was always at his best against the Yankees. He seemed to find a way to beat them, no matter what. He finished with a career mark of 27–13 against New York. Against everybody else he was only 101–103.

The Tigers lost the opener of the Independence Day doubleheader to Whitey Ford. But Lary was on the mound in the second game, and he was in the midst of a 23-win season, his best ever. This game was one of his classics for several reasons.

He had the Yanks shut out until Maris reached him for a two-run homer in the eighth to tie the game 2–2. Then in the ninth, Detroit pulled off a triple steal, with shortstop Chico Fernandez swiping home on the front end to give Lary the lead again. But once more the Yankees fought back to tie it in their half.

The Tigers put runners on third and second with two outs in the tenth. Lary was allowed to bat for himself, a rather unorthodox

LOST TO THE WAR

There were several Tigers whose career stats were deeply impacted by World War II. Certainly Hank Greenberg was foremost, missing four full seasons after averaging 39 homers in the previous six.

There was also Dick Wakefield, who hit .316 and .355 in 233 big-league games before entering the service at the age of 23, and never came anywhere near .300 again. Barney McCosky averaged .317 in his first four years with the Tigers and lost three seasons at the age of 24. Catcher Birdie Tebbetts also lost three seasons at the age of 29, and Virgil Trucks was gone for two prime years at 24.

move by Scheffing. But the manager knew that his pitcher was also a superb bunter. Lary laid down a perfect squeeze bunt, bringing in the run that won the game. He now had beaten the Yankees in almost every way possible. But the denouement was yet to come.

Detroit returned to Yankee Stadium on another holiday, a Labor Day weekend series. The Yankees were one and a half games ahead, and everyone knew this was it. The Tigers had their three top starters lined up, and Don Mossi got the call against Ford in the Friday night game. It was Yankee Stadium at its most intimidating, with a capacity crowd and four decades of tradition looking on.

When Ford had to leave the game in the fifth with a strained hip muscle, it seemed the Tigers had been given their chance. But Buddy Daley was called in and the knuckleballer had enough to keep the Tigers off balance. It was still 0–0 into the eighth.

Detroit had opportunities all night long. Two Tigers had been picked off first. When Bruton walked with one out in the eighth, Al Kaline rifled a drive into the treacherous left-field corner. Yogi Berra, inexperienced in the outfield, was playing out there, and it seemed Bruton might even be able to score.

But the ball caromed perfectly off the wall—right into Yogi's glove. When Kaline tried for a double, he was thrown out. At that point, the Tigers probably knew their fate was sealed.

Mossi had a five-hitter going into the last of the ninth, and when he disposed of both Maris and Mantle, it seemed extra innings were a certainty. But Elston Howard grounded a single to center and Berra grounded one to right field. That brought up Bill Skowron, a dangerous right-handed hitter to face the left-handed Mossi. Scheffing kept him in the game and Skowron responded with dinky single number three, a simple ground ball through the left side.

The Yankees won 1–0 and broke Detroit's heart. Even Lary couldn't hold them off on Saturday, and the following day Howard smashed a three-run shot in the last of the ninth to complete the sweep.

The race was over. Although they won 101 games, the Tigers finished eight lengths behind the overpowering Yankees. It took another seven long years before Detroit could finally retool and break through.

BARTELL HOLDS THE BALL (1940)

Dick Bartell played shortstop on three pennant-winning teams. He made the National League's All-Star squad a couple of times, hit over .300 on six occasions, and was regarded as one of the top hit-and-run men of his era. His nickname, Rowdy Richard, is a clue to the aggressive nature he brought to the game.

Yet he is remembered in Detroit for holding on to the ball in the 1940 World Series as the Reds rallied to win Game 7.

His frozen moment is not as famous a case of inaction as Johnny Pesky's would be six years later. That's probably because St. Louis's Enos Slaughter scored all the way from first on a double to beat the Red Sox when Pesky did not throw the relay to the plate. Cincinnati's runner merely came in from second with the tying run, but the ultimate damage was identical.

The underdog Reds won the game and the Series, 2–1. The Tigers could have snuffed out the winning rally, however, if Bartell had only thrown to the plate.

Detroit had traded the aging Billy Rogell to the Cubs in order to get him. It was regarded as an upgrade on defense. While he hit only .233 as a leadoff man, Bartell managed to get on base ahead of the big guns—Charlie Gehringer, Hank Greenberg, Barney McCosky, and Rudy York—and that's all the Tigers wanted. The Tigers were far and away the best hitting team in baseball and they didn't think they would have much of a problem with Cincinnati.

True enough, the Reds had won 100 games and breezed to the pennant while the Tigers had to fight to the last weekend of the season. They also had two 20-game winners in Bucky Walters and Paul Derringer. It was the best and deepest staff in the game.

The team's lone offensive threat, though, was first baseman Buck McCormick, who drove in 127 runs. Their other big hitter, catcher Ernie Lombardi, had gone down with a sprained ankle in September.

This presented a major problem. The backup catcher, Willard Hershberger, suffered from depression and, blaming himself for a critical loss in August, committed suicide in his Boston hotel room.

That left only 40-year-old bullpen coach Jimmie Wilson. He would have to start every game in the Series after playing in just seven games in the previous two years. Wilson was known as a smart receiver, the man who helped turn Dizzy Dean into a big-league pitcher. He also had managed the Phillies, one of the most thankless jobs in baseball at that time, for five years. It was asking a lot for him to step up now.

But the Reds would not roll over. Detroit's ace, Bobo Newsom, beat them twice. When facing elimination in Game 6, though, Walters throttled the Tigers 4–0 on just five hits. Wilson not only called a brilliant game, but was hitting a steady .267.

Newsom was ready to pitch Game 7 on just one day's rest, and Derringer, the Game 4 winner, would work for the Reds. The home fans were pessimistic. There were about 6,000 empty seats at Crosley Field as Cinci went for its first championship in 21 years.

The Tigers scored their only run on a throwing error by third baseman Billy Werber in the third. But that's all there was. Newsom had blanked the Reds in Game 5 and, apparently, he was going to have to do it again. The Tigers had their chances, but they couldn't break through on Derringer again.

In the seventh, McCormick, who had been held in check by the Tigers, slammed a double off the left-field wall. That brought Jimmy Ripple to the plate. He had played with Bartell on the pennant-winning 1937 Giants and came over to the Reds in a late-season deal. He also had been one of the most productive Cincinnati hitters in the Series, driving in a team-high five runs.

The Tigers expected a bunt that would send the tying run to third. It was the kind of small ball the Reds usually played. Ripple instead sent a high fastball on a line to deep right field. It seemed that Bruce Campbell had a chance to catch it, but the ball hit the wall just above his glove and landed right at his feet.

McCormick had gone back to tag up on the play. As Campbell whipped the ball in to Bartell, the lumbering Reds first baseman was barely rounding third. Bartell was known for his strong arm, and everyone in the park was screaming as McCormick kept chugging toward the plate. He seemed to be a certain out, a huge blow to Cinci.

But Bartell never made the throw. He never even turned around. While his teammates screamed at him, they couldn't be heard over the din.

"Bartell must have thought that he had no chance on McCormick with the ball hitting the wall like that," said Gehringer. "I was yelling 'Home. Home. Home.' With Bartell's arm, he [McCormick] was a dead pigeon. But he never threw, and by the time he looked, it was too late. To this day I don't know why."

Jimmie Wilson bunted Ripple to third, and shortstop Billy Myers picked him up with a long fly to center. That was the Series. Greenberg sent a screaming liner at Myers with one on in the eighth, but it was the last gasp—the Tigers never got another base runner.

Newsom was especially upset afterward. His father had passed away the night after Game 1, and he had dedicated Game 5 to him. He was asked whether he had wanted Game 7 for his dad, too.

"Naw, I wanted this one for Bobo," he said.

Newsom eventually got his championship ring with the 1947 Yankees. The aged Jimmie Wilson caught flawlessly and hit a stalwart .353 for the Series, and Bartell was released by the Tigers the following April. It had been a short but disarming stay in Detroit.

THE UGLY

COCHRANE GOES DOWN (1937)

The pitch came out of a wall of white shirts in the center-field stands on a blindingly bright May afternoon. It was doubtful that Mickey Cochrane even saw it until the last second.

Charlie Gehringer, who was in the on-deck circle, said the ball hit Cochrane on the temple and bounced halfway back to pitcher Bump Hadley. Cochrane crumpled to the ground and for the next four days struggled for his life with a compound skull fracture. He never played again.

The record shows that only one major leaguer, Ray Chapman, was killed after getting hit in the head. Others had their careers shortened or altered—Wally Moses, Joe Medwick, Tony Conigliaro.

Cochrane lived on for another 25 years after his beaning, but much of the man died inside that day.

Most of his contemporaries said he was the greatest catcher they ever saw, a flawless receiver who hit for a .320 lifetime average. Beyond the statistics, however, was the temperament he brought to the game. He occupied a place beyond aggressive, with a fiery will that not only refused to countenance defeat but rejected its very existence.

He played only 11 full seasons in the majors, and in five of them he went to the World Series. When the Tigers acquired him to be their playing manager in 1934, he transformed the ballclub and the city.

Despite getting up after being knocked unconscious by a pitch in 1937, Mickey Cochrane was never the same after the incident.

He was on the cover of *Time* magazine right after the Tigers won the 1935 Series. The profile said that: "His determined...face soon came to represent the picture of what a dynamic Detroiter ought to look like." His drive to win became a symbol of the city's recovery from the Great Depression.

Cochrane was a football star in high school and enrolled at Boston University to play. But he had to support his family and signed up for a minor league baseball team one summer under an assumed name. They made him a catcher and it took. Within two years he was behind the plate for Connie Mack's Philadelphia Athletics and became the anchor of two world championships.

But Mack had to sell his stars to stay in business during the Depression, including Lefty Grove, Jimmie Foxx, and Al Simmons. Cochrane was adored by the old man and was among the last to go.

The Tigers had finished a distant fifth in 1933. They did not have a reliable catcher, and manager Bucky Harris had been fired before the end of the season. Cochrane answered both of these needs. But no one could have anticipated how well.

Detroit tore through the league for the next two years, winning its first world championship driven by the indomitable leader in the mask. The Tigers hadn't won a pennant since 1909, and the place went slightly bonkers for Black Mike.

But in 1936 the formula stopped working. The Yankees, inspired by rookie Joe DiMaggio, burst out of the gate and gained an enormous lead over everyone else. Cochrane had been promoted to general manager by the team's new owner, Walter O. Briggs Sr. The added responsibilities, coupled with failure on the field and his own subpar performance at bat, was too much for his combative nature.

He suffered what was described as a nervous breakdown in late June and went off to a ranch in Wyoming to get it together. Hank Greenberg was also gone for the season, recovering from an injury suffered in the previous World Series. Without their two stars, the Tigers limped home, 19½ games behind the Yankees.

But in 1937 Cochrane was back, as was Greenberg, and things were going to be different. In late May the team went into Yankee Stadium only one and a half games off the lead. Schoolboy Rowe started against Hadley, and the Tigers had to like that matchup.

Hadley was 32, one year younger than Cochrane. He was no wild-eyed rookie but still threw hard after 11 seasons in the majors. In an odd juxtaposition of events, it was Hadley who had given up the last hit of Ty Cobb's career when he played with Cochrane on the A's in 1928.

By some accounts Cochrane threw up his hand to ward off the pitch. But Gehringer insisted Cochrane never saw the ball at all. There were no batting helmets in those days, no protection against a high, hard one that got away. Cochrane escaped death by only a matter of inches. (Chapman had been killed in a game against the Yankees in 1920, when the team still played at the Polo Grounds.)

Playing again was out of the question. Without being able to take his place on the field, Cochrane was a different man. The fires were not extinguished, but they had been banked.

He tried it in 1938, strictly as a bench manager. But his duties as general manager got in the way. He had purchased his old friend Simmons in 1936 and it hadn't worked out. Rowe went down with a sore arm the following year and, desperate for pitching help, Cochrane obtained Vern Kennedy from the White Sox. But he had to give up two fan favorites from the championship years, Gee Walker and Marv Owen, to do so.

The Tigers couldn't even get to .500 as the season wore on into August. Many of the other heroes were gone, too, and their replacements didn't measure up. Cochrane's on-field replacement, Rudy York, was hitting lots of homers but was a disaster as a catcher.

The fans who had cheered him wildly as the city's savior less than three years before turned on Cochrane now. He was fired by Briggs in August. He worked only briefly in the majors again, when the aged Mack, in his final year with the A's, hired him as general manager in 1950.

He spent most of his last years at a ranch he owned at the base of the mountains in Montana. Cochrane had always been a great one for climbing mountains.

ROCKY'S REVENGE (1968)

Detroit was not a happy stop for Rocky Colavito.

In Cleveland he was a civic icon. He had the sculpted good looks that made young girls swoon. In just four seasons he knocked out 129 homers, and the fans went wild when he came to bat. The Indians had made a strong pennant run in 1959, and Rocky led the league with 42 homers.

And then suddenly, inexplicably, it was over. Traded to the Tigers at the end of the next spring training—and for Harvey Kuenn, a singles hitter, for heaven's sake. Chortled Cleveland's general manager Frank Lane, "I traded a hamburger for a steak." That didn't help matters at all.

Colavito would not be the main man in Detroit. That distinction was reserved for Al Kaline. The Rock may have batted cleanup in the batting order, but he was a distinct second in the pecking order.

As fate would have it, the season opened at the big lakefront stadium in Cleveland, and 52,000 people came out to watch

Rocky's return. It was quite a performance. He came to bat six times, striking out in four of his at-bats, and hitting into a double play. The Tigers won anyway in 15 innings, but it wasn't the sort of debut they were hoping for.

That would come three days later, when the Tigers opened at home before their own crowd of 50,000. It was a glorious afternoon, one of the rare times Detroit ever greeted the baseball season in shirtsleeve weather.

On his very first time at bat in Detroit as a member of the Tigers, Colavito rifled a two-run shot into the left-field upper deck. The crowd went berserk.

But Rocky had a subpar season. Even in 1961, when he hit career highs with 45 homers and 140 RBIs, he was never fully embraced in Detroit. Colavito thrived on being in the spotlight. He craved admiration. It galled him that no matter what he accomplished, no matter how many fans he put in the seats, he could never be Kaline.

He had a great throwing arm but was one of the slowest runners in the league and only an adequate outfielder. And when he campaigned for a big raise, he was pointedly reminded that Kaline was the best-paid player on the team, and he made less than $100,000.

"What is Kaline," he responded, "a little tin god?"

That offhand remark sealed his fate in Detroit. He had blasphemed; as long as his numbers stayed high, that could be tolerated, but by 1963 he had fallen off to a weak 22 home runs, and the fans and media would not allow him to forget what he had said.

During the off-season he was exiled to Kansas City. The deal actually strengthened the Tigers because it brought second baseman Jerry Lumpe and pitcher Dave Wickersham in return. Rocky quickly faded from Motown's memory as new heroes arrived in the outfield from the farm system.

By 1968 he was a faded shadow of himself. He was with the Yankees, his fourth team in less than two seasons, and was barely hitting .200. That's where the Tigers encountered him when they arrived in New York for a four-game series in late August.

FELLER WHIFFS

The press box was full at Cleveland Stadium for the season-ending doubleheader in 1938. Both teams were out of the race. But Hank Greenberg was stuck on 58 homers, two short of the record Babe Ruth had set 11 years before.

Instead, the crowd saw another record fall. Nineteen-year-old Bob Feller struck out 18 Tigers in the first game, the highest mark ever at that time. He got Chet Laabs five times. Even though the Tigers won the game 4–1, Greenberg never came close to a homer.

A legend has started that Greenberg was deliberately thwarted by opposing teams who started a succession of wild rookie pitchers against the Tigers in the season's last week, but the facts don't support that. Only two times in the last two weeks did a rookie start, including the season finale.

Greenberg was facing veterans almost all the time. He just couldn't get the right pitches.

It was a typical sweltering summer heat wave in the city, and the Tigers were without their sparkplug, Dick McAuliffe. The leadoff man was serving a suspension after a fight with Chicago pitcher Tommy John. Mac had charged the mound after a pitch came unacceptably close, and in the scuffle John's pitching shoulder was injured. The league suspended McAuliffe for five games, until the team's last series of the year with the White Sox was over. But first there was the matter of the Yankees.

The Tigers had a cushy seven-and-a-half-game lead over Baltimore. They had breezed through the season without a substantial slump, and the Yankees, mired in sixth place, did not appear to be much of a threat.

But on Friday night, they lost the opener of a twi-night doubleheader occasioned by a rainout earlier in the year. The second game dragged on for 19 innings over five hours and was ended by the curfew at 1:00 AM. The Yankees tied it in the eighth, and veteran Lindy McDaniel came in and threw seven perfect innings. Without McAuliffe at the top of the order, the Tigers looked listless, wilted.

It got worse on Saturday. Denny McLain, with 25 wins under his belt, lost the game 2–1 on a first-inning homer by Roy White. Now they had another doubleheader on Sunday to make up for Friday's suspended game.

It was hot, both pitching staffs were exhausted, the hitters weren't producing, and the Orioles, playing at home against Oakland, were charging. But the bats came alive on Sunday, and the Tigers ran up a 5–0 lead. With no one else available, Yankees manager Ralph Houk decided to bring in Colavito to pitch relief. What was there to lose? Rocky liked to fool around during pregame warm-ups, pretending that he was a pitcher and trying to break off a curve along with his hard fastballs. He actually had pitched three innings for Cleveland back in 1958. But this was a pennant race and it was also the Tigers. That was a big difference.

Colavito came into the game in the fourth and got Kaline on a grounder. Then he pitched a scoreless fifth and sixth, giving up just one hit—to Kaline, naturally.

In the bottom of the sixth, disaster. With two outs, Willie Horton lost a fly ball in the blinding sunlight, and it bounced off his head for a double. Before order could be restored, the Yankees had scored five times and had the lead, 6–5. The final run of the rally was scored by Colavito.

The lead held up, and Rocky had his first and only big-league pitching win. Thoroughly demoralized, the Tigers lost the second game of the doubleheader, too. The big lead over Baltimore had been chopped to five, and the locker room was like a tomb.

When the team came in from the field, this message was written on a chalkboard: "Anyone who thinks the world ended today doesn't belong in this room." It had been scrawled by Eddie Mathews, who had been through a few pennant races and knew about bumps in the road.

The Tigers recovered their stride once they left New York and continued on to the pennant. Colavito was brought into the media area between games of the doubleheader to chortle slightly. He was released at the end of the season and never played in the majors again.

But on one muggy Sunday, Rocky had his measure of revenge.

UMPIRE PROBLEMS (1972, 1984)

It didn't take Billy Martin long as a manager to become the focus of hatred for most American League umpires. This sentiment was also widely shared by those who played for him.

When he was named to lead the Tigers in 1971, it was regarded as a desperation move. The team that won the Series in 1968 had grown complacent under the easygoing style of Mayo Smith. The front office was convinced this group had another pennant in them, and Martin was brought in to extract it, by force if necessary.

Martin had made a cameo appearance with the Tigers as an unsuccessful shortstop in 1958. He always had a reputation as a combative individual, to put it mildly. A nightclub brawl got him traded from the sedate Yankees in 1957. When he got his chance to manage Minnesota in 1969, he lasted just one year. Even though he won the divisional title, no one with the Twins organization could stand him. Their displeasure was heightened when he knocked out one of his pitchers in a discussion on baseball etiquette outside the famed Detroit sports hangout, the Lindell AC.

Martin's methods did produce some short-term results. The Tigers showed a 12-game improvement under his guidance in 1971 and even gave the Orioles a few anxious moments before the race was decided.

But in 1972 things came to a head. With a ballclub that consisted almost entirely of veterans, Martin never let up. To a few of the older Tigers it seemed he was quick to claim credit when things went right and to shift blame when they didn't. They fought off a strong challenge from Boston all summer, and it seemed that they had unified to fight off Martin, too.

"He put us in a frame of mind that took all the fun out of the game," said outfielder Jim Northrup. "When it's no fun, it's not worth playing."

Jim Evans, who was then a young umpire, said that much of Martin's motivational technique was based on intimidation, and he played off the umpires to build on that. "I respected him as a manager," said Evans, "but there were times he showed utter disrespect for the game."

Most of the Tigers who played in the fifth and final game of the 1972 playoffs were convinced that the umpires got some of that respect back. John Rice, regarded as a solid 18-year veteran, was stationed at first base. He was a hard-nosed guy who carried a tape measure in his pocket to make sure batters were staying within the rules when they stood at the plate. He brooked no guff.

There was a violent outburst in Game 2 when Tigers pitcher Lerrin Lagrow and Oakland's Bert Campaneris had a severe disagreement. Lagrow plunked him with a pitch, Campaneris threw his bat at the pitcher, and then he ran to the mound to engage him directly. Both players were suspended for the rest of the playoffs, but the loss of their shortstop was much more critical to the A's. Martin, nonetheless, was convinced that the umpiring crew had it in for him, and his heckling from the dugout was merciless.

In the fourth inning of the fifth game, in a 1–1 tie, A's leadoff hitter George Hendrick sent a grounder to second base. The throw to first was a bit high, and Norm Cash had to stretch for it, but the ball clearly beat Hendrick to the bag. Rice called him safe, ruling that Cash had come off the bag too soon.

The Tigers protested violently, and televised replays seemed to confirm that Hendrick was out. Cash conceded later that even if he had left the bag quickly to avoid being spiked, that call was never made on such a play. He was convinced Rice made it only because he hated Martin. In an indication of how bitterly aggrieved they were, in later years some of the players even suggested darker motives involving gambling, but nothing was ever proven.

Hendrick came around to score on a single to left, where Martin had decided to play Duke Sims. Sims was normally a catcher and had played fewer than 50 games in the outfield in his career. He charged the ball clumsily, and his throw to the plate was late. The final score was 2–1, and those two plays decided the pennant.

Martin, trying to deflect criticism of his own strategy, went off on Rice. But his players knew the bad call was only half the problem. Martin lasted only one more year in Detroit.

It took 12 more seasons, but Tigers fans saw the bar of umpiring justice right itself rather painfully. Larry Barnett really had done nothing to antagonize the Tigers when he was working home plate in the second game of the 1984 World Series. But he got it anyhow.

Aurelio Lopez was pitching in relief for the Tigers in the fifth inning, trying to squelch a winning three-run rally by the Padres. His nickname was Señor Smoke, an indication of how hard he could throw.

With a runner on first, catcher Lance Parrish flashed the sign for a pitchout. "Lopez sometimes had problems picking up the signs," said Parrish. "But he nodded right away as if he got this one, and I set up for an outside pitch. He threw a fastball right down the middle."

The batter took it, and Parrish had no chance to get his glove back. So the ball struck Barnett right where the pain is the greatest, about halfway down the crotch.

Barnett doubled over in agony while Parrish ran out to the mound in disbelief. "I saw the sign," Lopez told Parrish, "but the ball got away from me." Parrish said that the pitcher's eyes were almost bugging out in distress.

"I ran back to Barnett to see how he was," said the catcher, "and I kept apologizing, letting him know that it was not intentional. I must have apologized to him every time I saw him for the next year. You don't want an umpire carrying a grudge."

As for Barnett, he claimed the incident was a natural opener for him at speaking engagements. Because it happened during the World Series, his moment of agony was witnessed by a national TV audience. Barnett would say that it was the only time in history an umpire had to call a strike and two balls on the same pitch.

DENNY CHECKS OUT (1970)

Denny McLain always knew how to make a big splash. But who could have imagined that the final chapter of his career with the Tigers would include dumping pails of water over the heads of two baseball writers?

What a scamp.

Denny McLain was at the peak of his game in 1968, becoming the first pitcher to win 30 games since Dizzy Dean accomplished the same feat in 1934.

For two wild seasons in the late 1960s, McLain was the greatest show in baseball, if not on Earth. In 1968 he became the first pitcher in 34 years to win 30 games. Dizzy Dean had been the last to do it in 1934, and prior to that only Lefty Grove and Jim Bagby had reached the mark after the dead-ball era.

Win number 30 had come just days before the Tigers clinched their first pennant in 23 years, and the city knew no greater hero. If McLain had told the adoring crowds to stop the cheering and throw money at him instead, they would have gladly complied.

He followed that up with winning the Cy Young Award for a second straight season. At 24–9, his record wasn't quite as spectacular as it had been in the previous campaign, but it was good enough for a league-leading nine shutouts and top-five finishes in most other categories.

McLain had pitched 661 innings over those two years, an absolutely astounding total by contemporary standards. Even more impressive, out of the 82 times he started, he pitched 51 complete games. This was a time before designated hitters and closers and set-up men and quality starts being defined as six innings of work. The numbers are a true indication of how radically the game has changed since 1969.

Even by those standards, however, McLain was a horse. Back-to-back 300-inning seasons take a toll, and McLain was getting cortisone shots in his right arm on a regular basis. That explains the problems with his arm, but not his head.

It was an open secret in Detroit that he was involved with bookies and had placed bets on basketball games from the clubhouse telephone in Lakeland, Florida. Nasty rumors still swirled around his mysterious injury during the 1967 pennant race. Respected *Detroit News* columnist Pete Waldmeir had written that McLain was stomped by a local mafioso as a form of late-payment fee on some losing bets.

It all came down during the winter of 1970. The commissioner's office announced it was suspending McLain until July after investigating the gambling allegations. It had determined that he was not only making bets, he was also taking them in his own bookmaking operation. It was a stunning reversal of fortune. The man who had been the toast of the town was now just toast.

With their top pitcher gone, the Tigers, just two years removed from a championship, were a team near collapse. Mickey Lolich would go on to lose 19 games, while the next two spots in the rotation were held down by the likes of Les Cain and Joe Niekro. Manager Mayo Smith could do nothing to rally the troops and, indeed, they had tuned him out. The loose reins with which he had run the team before could not be tightened. Even members of the Tigers admitted they had quit on him and, in the words of Jim Northrup, "laid down like dogs."

Still, when July began there was the hope that when Denny came back, somehow, someway, the team would catch fire. On July 1 that still wasn't implausible. They were within reach of Baltimore, just seven games behind. Mayo could hardly wait to start McLain that night against the Yankees. Almost 54,000 fans packed Tiger Stadium to see McLain's season debut. He only made it to the sixth inning before being relieved, giving up five runs, but the Tigers rallied to win 6–5 in 11 innings. He pitched much better against the first place Orioles at Baltimore on July 5, a 2–0 loss that seemed to be encouraging, indicating that he could still pitch at a high level.

His next start came in the second game of a doubleheader against Baltimore one week later. Again, more than 50,000 people

PHILLY MASSACRE

When Ty Cobb went into the stands in New York in May 1912 to attack a vicious heckler who happened to have lost part of his hand in an accident, American League president Ban Johnson decided that he'd seen enough. He immediately suspended the Tigers star.

Cobb's teammates decided that was unfair and refused to take the field against Philadelphia. Wanting to avoid a fine for forfeiting the game, the Tigers rounded up a bunch of local sandlot players and college students to take on the mighty A's, who trampled them 24–2. The point was taken, and while Johnson sputtered in rage, he eventually lifted the suspension.

packed Tiger Stadium, all of them hoping to see the once and future Denny. He couldn't get out of the fourth, however, and the Orioles blasted Detroit 13–3.

The old McLain had not shown up. But even the most pessimistic fan couldn't have guessed that he would win just three more games for the Tigers and 17 in his entire major league career. He would finish just one of his 14 starts that summer and give up more than four and a half runs a game. There would be no quick revival. Not this year, and as it was becoming increasingly apparent, maybe not ever. The cortisone was only a palliative measure for the pain. He was just 26 years old, but all those innings had burned his arm out.

The frustrations mounted, and by late August McLain decided that it was all the fault of the media. Weren't they the ones who were always criticizing, asking questions, running negative stories? There were beat reporters with the Tigers from each of the city's two dailies. Watson Spoelstra of the *News* was a veteran and had been covering the team for almost two decades. Jim Hawkins of the *Free Press* was in his first year.

McLain waited until they got to the clubhouse one afternoon, motioned them over to his locker, and dumped a pail of water on each of them. In his mind it was only a prank. It was Denny being Denny. Hawkins was young and might have laughed it off. But Spoelstra was enraged. He went to general manager Jim Campbell, sputtering in anger and demanding something be done about it.

To Campbell, this was the final proof that McLain had gone permanently around the bend. He immediately suspended him for the rest of the year. As soon as the season was finished, he wrapped up McLain and suckered Washington into a preposterous deal. The Tigers got two great defensive infielders, Aurelio Rodriguez and Eddie Brinkman, and a big-time starting pitcher in Joe Coleman Jr. They became part of the nucleus that won the divisional title in 1972.

McLain lasted one year in Washington and lost 22 games. After one more year, with the A's and the Braves, it was over. Washed up at 28.

Denny's life quickly spiraled out of control. There were bankruptcies and a federal racketeering charge in Florida that landed him in prison. Although he had ballooned to more than 300 pounds, he returned to Detroit in the 1980s and managed to rebuild his life as a successful radio talk-show host. Then he acquired an out-of-state meat-packing company, was charged with blowing out its pension fund, and went back to prison a second time.

The long joyride had turned into one of the ugliest extended episodes in Tigers history.

THROWN AWAY (2006)

The unexpected pennant earned by the 2006 Tigers was such an exhilarating, semimystical experience that it may seem churlish to carp about what happened in the World Series. However, there

In the 2006 World Series against the St. Louis Cardinals, the Tigers committed eight errors with five by the pitchers, including this one by Todd Jones.

is a distinct difference between getting beaten and throwing it away. Unfortunately, the Tigers did the latter.

In the five games with the Cardinals, the Tigers committed a horrendous eight errors. Five were by the pitchers, a record, and three of them involved unforced wild throws. If this had been the NBA Finals, you'd have to say that turnovers made the difference. But turnovers are expected in basketball—not so much in baseball.

In 1945, usually described as the worst Series ever played, the Tigers made five errors. But it took them seven whole games to do that, and they did emerge as the winners. Every one of the Detroit errors this time led to St. Louis runs, and almost all of them came during game-deciding rallies. It was an ugly end to a sweet season.

The Tigers had gone into the Series as heavy favorites thanks to a 7–1 run through the playoffs against the Yankees and the A's. They had lost the Central Division lead by one game to Minnesota on the last day of the season. Still, their 95 wins were 12 better than St. Louis, which had one of the weakest winning percentages in Series history.

But the pattern was set right at the outset. The Cards went off to an early 4–1 lead in Game 1 at Comerica Park, thanks to a two-run shot by Albert Pujols. Justin Verlander, at the climax of a great rookie year, kept Detroit within comeback distance for a while. But in the sixth, it all imploded.

Verlander walked Pujols to start off. He had one of the best pickoff moves in the game for a right-hander, a fact of which Pujols was apparently unaware. Verlander had him caught off the bag cold, but then fired the ball past first baseman Sean Casey into the right-field corner. This seemed to rattle the rookie, and two quick hits followed, making it 5–1.

Juan Encarnacion then sent a grounder at Brandon Inge, who knocked it down with his chest and then made another wild throw to first. One run scored, and another followed when Inge was called for obstruction for standing in the baseline. That made two errors on one play, three for the inning, and the game was already out of hand.

Detroit won Game 2, 3–1, but even in victory the pitcher had a problem. Closer Todd Jones fumbled a grounder that would have ended the game, and it gave the Cards their only run. Most of Jones's closing efforts resembled thrill rides anyhow, and this one was no different. He closed it out, but that was pitcher error number two.

The third was far more damaging. In Game 3, with St. Louis ahead only 2–0 in the seventh, Joel Zumaya, another of Detroit's overachieving rookies, walked the first two men in the inning. Pujols then sent one back to the mound, and Zumaya inexplicably decided the play was at third. The ball sailed wildly past the startled Inge, two runners scored, and then *that* game was out of hand.

The Tigers were still in it, though, and went into the seventh inning of Game 4 with a 3–2 lead. Then it started getting spooky. Leadoff man David Eckstein sent a liner to center, and in an eerie

FORGETTABLE DEBUT

Opening Day 2000 was as eagerly anticipated as any in Detroit history. It was the first to be played in Comerica Park, the new facility near the heart of the city's downtown. Even the team's 1–5 start on the road couldn't dampen enthusiasm for the stadium that was billed as a vital piece of the city's revitalization.

But April 11 was bitterly cold, a windy day with temperatures only in the upper 30s. Walks, errors, and balks dragged out the first three innings to well over an hour. Even with the Tigers leading 4–0, fans started leaving in droves.

Moreover, the stadium was not yet ready for prime time. There were interminable waits at the concession stands. Spectators in the lower boxes complained that the pitch of the stands was so slight that their view of the field was obscured. But they could clearly see the forbidding outfield distances that necessitated a drastic realignment of the fences. It got better, but the opener was definitely a dud.

replay of Curt Flood's stumble in the 1968 Series with the Cards, Detroit's Curtis Granderson fell down and couldn't regain his footing in time. It went as a hit, but everyone knows you can't defend against bad karma. And it went from bad to worse in a hurry.

Reliever Fernando Rodney picked up a sacrifice bunt and flung it over the head of second baseman Placido Polanco. Eckstein came in to tie the game, and two outs later Preston Wilson picked up the go-ahead run with a single. The Cards held on, 5–4. They had blown open all three of their wins because of throwing errors. They weren't done yet, either.

With Detroit ahead 2–1 in the fourth inning of Game 5, Verlander uncorked yet another errant throw. It came on a bunt with two runners on, and this fifth error by a Detroit pitcher led to the runs that put the Cards ahead to stay. Series over.

The Detroit hitters, with the exception of Casey, were held in check for almost the entire Series. That certainly was a factor in the inglorious defeat. Some also were inclined to blame the week-long delay between the time the Tigers clinched the pennant and when the Series actually began. It gave the Tigers rookies, and several other regulars who had never experienced the postseason before, time to sit around and realize where they were.

But manager Jim Leyland refused to accept any excuses. Accountability was his mantra all year long, and he wouldn't abandon it now, even as he saw one game after another thrown out the window.

IN THE CLUTCH

BOSS SCHMIDT'S COLLAPSE (1907)

It wasn't as if the Tigers weren't forewarned. In each of the three years they went on to the World Series with Boss Schmidt as Detroit's starting catcher, Schmidt led the American League in errors. He made a total of 91, an appalling number for someone playing that position—although passed balls were counted as errors under the rules then in effect.

By comparison, Johnny Kling, the catcher for the Cubs and Schmidt's opposite number in two of those Series, led the National League in fielding and made a total of only 24 errors in those seasons.

White Sox catcher Billy Sullivan had predicted before the 1907 Series that catching would be the difference. The Cubs would run wild on Schmidt, Sullivan said, and the Tigers wouldn't be able to do it on Kling. No one knew how wild it would get—not just in that Series, but in the next two, which the Tigers also lost.

There are many reasons the Tigers hold the distinction of being just one of two teams in major league history to lose three World Series in a row. (The other was the New York Giants of 1911–1913.)

Ty Cobb hit 105 points below his lifetime average in these games. The Detroit pitching staff was overmatched. The infield defense couldn't compare to the legendary Chicago combination of Tinker to Evers to Chance, nor to Pittsburgh's great shortstop Honus Wagner.

But Schmidt certainly didn't help matters.

He had come to the majors a few months after Cobb and immediately won the admiration of his teammates by thrashing the abrasive young star in a fistfight. Schmidt hailed from a town in Arkansas called Coal Hill and he was every bit as tough as that name implies. He stood around 6' tall and was a rock-hard 200

Despite having Ty Cobb (pictured above) on the team, the Tigers fell apart against the Chicago Cubs in the 1907 World Series. Photo courtesy of Getty Images.

pounds. Teammates swore he could drive nails into a board with his bare fist.

He just had some failings as a catcher. The opposition stole 49 bases on the Tigers in 17 games in those three World Series matchups. To make it even worse, Schmidt's cumulative Series batting average was .159. There has rarely been a weaker performance in the clutch.

His very worst moment came in the first Series game he caught in 1907.

The Cubs were regarded as the greatest team of the era. They won 107 games that year and came into the Series angry. There was some evening-up to attend to. In the previous season they had won a record 116 games but were upset in the Series by their crosstown rivals, the White Sox, a team so feeble at the plate that it became known throughout history as the Hitless Wonders.

Cubs Manager Frank Chance was determined this would not come close to happening again, and the Cubs were overwhelming favorites. They could start five pitchers who had earned-run averages of under 2.00. Chance chose his top winner, Orvie Overall (23–7), to start the opener against Wild Bill Donovan.

It turned out to be a great duel, as Overall made a fourth-inning run stand up. Detroit had its chances, but Kling picked two runners off third to kill rallies. The Tigers finally broke through in the top half of the eighth. The Cubs made three errors, two of them by the usually dependable Joe Tinker and Kling. Sam Crawford came through with a big hit, and the Tigers vaulted into the lead, 3–1. That's where it stood going into the last of the ninth.

The Chicago fans stirred uneasily. It was happening again with these American League upstarts. But the Tigers seemed determined to hand the game right back to the Cubs.

A single, a hit batsman, and a mishandled bunt by third baseman Bill Coughlin loaded the bases with one out. Donovan got the dangerous Wildfire Schulte on a grounder. A runner scored, making it 3–2, but all the Cubs had in reserve to bat for the weak-hitting Tinker was utility man Del Howard.

Donovan was Detroit's most dependable pitcher, a 31-year-old veteran who had gone 25–4 during the season. Howard presented no problem to him, even with the tying run on third. On a 2–2 count, he broke off a tremendous curveball. Howard swung futilely, and the Tigers seemed to have won the opener 3–2.

But wait a minute. The ball was trickling away from Schmidt, and Harry Steinfeldt was dashing in from third with the run that tied the game. At the most critical moment of his career, Schmidt had failed to hold on to a third strike. He claimed later that it was a foul tip, although no one else on the field saw it that way.

The teams struggled on for three more innings before the game was halted by darkness. It went down as a 3–3 tie, and the Series would start all over again the next day.

After that, the Tigers never had a chance. Given a reprieve, the Cubs stomped all over them, winning four in a row while the Tigers could manage a total of only three runs. Chicago leadoff man Jimmy Slagle, whose nickname was Rabbit, swiped six bases, a Series record that would stand up for 60 years, until Lou Brock broke it.

"All that talk of what Cobb was going to do made us sick," Slagle said afterward. "They lost heart when they found they couldn't run and didn't play up to the teaching of [manager Hughie] Jennings."

It was almost as bad the next year. The Tigers did manage to win a game, but then were shut out in the final two and lost the Series in five. The Bennett Park crowd of 6,210 at the closer remains the lowest attendance ever at a World Series game.

The following year, Pittsburgh completed the trifecta and stole 21 bases in seven games. Jennings stood loyally, some might say stubbornly, by his beleaguered catcher. But after this third straight failure, he'd seen enough. Oscar Stanage was brought in as the regular catcher in 1910. Too late. The Tigers would never return to the Series under Jennings, and in one more year Schmidt's playing career was over.

The Tigers never held it against him, though. Schmidt passed away in 1932, but 37 years later, when the Detroit organization learned that his grave in Arkansas was unmarked, it provided the money to buy their old catcher a headstone.

TANANA'S GEM (1987)

The Tigers were dead. Anyone could see that. Blowing a two-run lead to first-place Toronto in the last of the ninth with just one week left in the season...you don't come back from something like that.

After that late rally, the Blue Jays had a three-and-a-half-game lead over the Tigers with eight left to play. They had beaten Detroit three in a row. But what happened over the next week ranks among the greatest clutch performances in Tigers history.

It isn't all that well remembered because Detroit had nothing left for the playoffs, and the underdog Twins steamrollered them in five games. But the Tigers' stretch run was a classic, and it culminated in a 1–0 win on the final Sunday of the season by hometown hero Frank Tanana.

He once had been a big winner, a power pitcher with California. Teaming with Nolan Ryan, he was part of the top starting combination in the American League. But that had been a decade ago. Since then Tanana had suffered with arm problems. He also had been nicknamed Tanana Daiquiri by ESPN's Chris Berman, and there was more than a splash of truth to that. Tanana

Pitcher Frank Tanana helped lead his hometown team to a memorable comeback in 1987.

admitted that too many happy hours when he was at the top of his game had helped bring him down.

He was dealt to Boston, then to Texas, where he never had a winning season and was acquired by the Tigers in 1985. He was then 32 years old, and the arm that once struck out 17 hitters in a game was just a memory. But he was a more complete pitcher, the crafty southpaw of the great baseball cliché—a junk pitcher relying on control, or as Tigers catcher Matt Nokes phrased it, "A poo chucker." He also had attained inner peace through a religious rebirth. And in 1987 he turned out to be an essential ingredient of a contending staff.

But by late September that didn't seem to matter much. One more hard shove by the Blue Jays and the teetering Tigers would be knocked flat. It looked like the final push would be administered by Tom Henke. He was the top closer in the league, a pitcher so overpowering at the endgame that he was nicknamed the Terminator, after the Arnold Schwarzenegger movie character.

He came in to protect a 1–0 lead in the last game of the series in Toronto. With three outs to go, it was as sure a deal as these things get. But Kirk Gibson led off the ninth with another of his clutch homers, and in the thirteenth he cracked an RBI single for the win. The Tigers had escaped extinction, but Toronto's magic number was only five.

"We're either on borrowed time or we're setting the biggest bear trap in history," said Gibson after the series. It appeared to be the former, as the Tigers could do no better than split with Baltimore, with Tanana winning his 14th game of the season. But suddenly the Jays were reeling. They lost three in a row to Milwaukee and came into Tiger Stadium for the season finale with their lead pared down to one game.

Doyle Alexander won his ninth straight on Friday night, and now the two teams were tied. Whoever swept would win the division, while a split would mean a one-game playoff. In a tense Saturday game, Jack Morris and Mike Flanagan went through nine innings with a 2–2 tie.

Flanagan, a former Cy Young Award winner with Baltimore, had stopped the Tigers and Morris the previous weekend in

Toronto. But after 11 innings he had reached his limit, and the Jays were forced to make a change. That opened the door. The Tigers loaded the bases against the Toronto bullpen, and Alan Trammell delivered a single for the win.

Now it was Sunday and it was the Tigers, astonishingly, who were in control. The Jays had lost six in a row. One more and their season was over. But they had their ace, 17-game-winner Jimmy Key, ready to go against Tanana.

Tanana had been a local star at Catholic Central, a standout in basketball as well as baseball. As a kid he had come to Tiger Stadium to root for his favorite team. Now here he was, many years later, with 51,000 people in the stands, and he was living out the dream of his boyhood—one game for the divisional pennant.

With one out in the second, Larry Herndon homered to give the Jays a 1–0 lead. That's all they would get. From there on, Key gave up just one more hit. The rest was up to Tanana.

Again and again the Jays would put runners in scoring position. Tanana turned them away every time. Once he wild-pitched

THE SLAMMER HIMSELF

Nothing defines hitting in the clutch like a grand slam home run, and Jim Northrup knew the drill. He hit four during the 1968 season and followed it up with a fifth in the World Series. But his biggest impact came with the first two, which were hit in consecutive innings of the same game.

Slam number one broke open a 3–2 game at Cleveland on June 24. The Indians had walked Willie Horton on purpose to load the bases in the fifth and get deeper into the lineup. Northrup was batting seventh because a left-hander had started for Cleveland. But after reliever Eddie Fisher struck out Don Wert, Northrup connected, and it was 7–2.

In the next inning the bases filled again on a double and two hit batters. When new pitcher Billy Rohr came in, the first man he faced was Northrup. Same result. The Tigers won 14–3, and the legend of the Slammer was born.

a base runner to second, and another time a runner reached base when Tanana threw a wild pitch on strike three. Nothing fazed him. They couldn't break through.

Cecil Fielder (then the Jays' first baseman and three years away from becoming a star in Detroit) ripped a one-out single in the fourth and then, oddly enough, was thrown out trying to steal second. One of the slowest men in the big leagues, Fielder had only two steals in his entire career. Since Manny Lee followed with a triple, it was a critical turn of events. But Tanana left Lee standing at third. After that sequence, it was easy to believe that the final outcome may have been fated. As the ninth began, the crowd was up and screaming nervously for Tanana to get three more.

The always-dangerous Fielder struck out, and Lee grounded to third. That left Garth Iorg, and he tapped the ball right back to the mound. Tanana fired to first and then leaped in the air as the Tigers poured from the dugout.

One of the franchise's greatest clutch comebacks had been punctuated by one of its greatest clutch-pitching performances ever.

WILLIE'S THROW (1968)

The longest throw ever measured on a baseball diamond was uncorked by Sheldon LeJeune in Detroit. He was a minor league outfielder who fired a ball 467 feet in an exhibition against Cincinnati, from the base of the center-field fence to home plate.

Willie Horton's throw in the 1968 World Series probably didn't even travel half that distance. But when it comes to historic, there is nothing like it in all the Tigers' annals. It turned the Series around. From that moment on, it was all Detroit in a Series that had seemed all but lost.

Ironically, Horton often was taken out of games for defensive reasons. His place in the majors was earned with his bat. His arm was regarded as barely adequate. But none of the 262 home runs he hit in his career with the Tigers had the impact of this one clutch throw. Funny how things work out.

Until the moment he was cut down at home by Horton's throw, Lou Brock had tormented the Tigers. They couldn't get him out, and, once he got on base, they couldn't hold him in. He had been outstanding in the St. Louis triumphs of 1964 and 1967, hitting .356 and setting the record for steals in one Series with seven.

This time he was even better. He had already tied his own record for steals, and it was only the fifth game. When he came to bat in the fifth inning, he was 10 for 18 and had driven in six runs as the leadoff man in the batting order. Catcher Bill Freehan couldn't begin to cope with him. To make it even worse, Freehan was hitless at the plate.

The Cards just needed to win this game to wrap it up, and Orlando Cepeda gave them a jump start toward that end by blasting a three-run homer off Mickey Lolich in the first. Brock, naturally, was on base at the time.

He also singled in the third, but in a rare reversal Freehan managed to throw him out on a steal. Maybe that was an omen. Then in the bottom of the fourth the Tigers managed to score twice, and the glum capacity crowd began to cheer up.

But with one out in the St. Louis fifth, here was that man again. Brock rifled a double off the left-field wall, his third straight hit off Lolich. That brought Julian Javier to the plate. The game and the entire Series—had reached a critical moment. After cutting into the Cards' lead, it was essential that Detroit hold them in the next half inning, and everyone in the ballpark knew it.

Brock edged off second, and Javier slapped a hard liner to left. The stadium sagged. The run was a gimme, and St. Louis would be up by two again. Everybody understood that but Horton.

"We'd been watching film and saw that Brock had got himself into some bad habits," he said later. "He was so used to National League left fielders conceding the run, he never slid into the plate. I saw that and I filed it away in my head."

Now the time was at hand to pull out that file. Third baseman Don Wert was positioned perfectly as the cutoff man. Horton lined him up and aimed the throw right between his eyes. It is doubtful that Wert could have heard a shouted call to let it go through, but by some instinct, that's what he did.

The ball came in one hop and seemed to get to Freehan a fraction of a second later than the flying Brock. Eight autumns before this, Freehan had been a big, physical end for the University of Michigan football team. He started two games and won his letter. There was no one who was going to crash through his block now, especially this man who had been making his life a misery. Freehan outweighed Brock by more than 30 pounds. When Brock put his foot down to touch the plate, he simply bounced off the catcher.

Freehan immediately whirled around and tagged Brock. Plate umpire Doug Harvey didn't hesitate. He thrust his arm up in the out sign.

Brock was furious, and the rest of the Cards came rushing out to protest. To the unaided eye, there was no way of telling whether he had been safe or out. Many spectators believed the Tigers actually had been given a break.

But repeated replays from every conceivable angle proved conclusively that Harvey got it right. Brock had never touched the plate. Under the greatest possible pressure, Horton had made the throw of a lifetime and ended the Cards threat. While it wasn't yet apparent, he had also changed everything.

From that moment on, Brock was a nuisance rather than a menace. He hit only .222 the rest of the Series, and the Tigers now would get the chance to dig into the soft underbelly of the St. Louis pitching staff. With one out and one on in the seventh, Cards manager Red Schoendienst called in his best reliever, left-hander Joe Hoerner. He had won eight games, saved 17 more, had a 1.48 earned-run average, and was now being asked to get eight more outs for the Series. He couldn't even get one.

Although Hoerner was supposed to be death on left-handed hitters, Dick McAuliffe managed to send a bad-hop single into right. Then Mickey Stanley walked, and the bases were loaded.

That brought Al Kaline to the plate, and here it was. He was now 33 years old and had been the face of the franchise for 13 seasons. He was idolized in Detroit; after his retirement, they would name a street after him. The huge crowd was standing, screaming, begging the man they had cheered for all these years to come through for them one more time.

The Tigers had taken an unbelievable gamble, starting their center fielder Stanley at shortstop, a position he had played in all of nine games, just to get Kaline into the lineup. He had missed 62 games this season after being hit by a pitch and had lost his starting job as the team raced on without him to a pennant. Everything had been ordered for this one moment.

Hoerner tried to work the outside of the plate, and Kaline slapped the pitch on a sinking line into right-center. The tying and lead runs came racing home, and the ballpark crowd went crazy, a deafening din unlike anything even the oldest fans could remember.

The Tigers never trailed in that Series again. They finished off that game with a 5–3 win and then swept the Cards in the last two in St. Louis. And none of it would have happened had it not been for Willie's throw.

GIEBELL'S GIFT (1940)

The lines barely add up to a blink in the pitchers section of the *Baseball Encyclopedia*. Sandwiched in between Joe Gideon and Paul Giel, they are easy to miss.

Floyd Giebell's entire major league career consisted of 28 games and three wins. But one of those wins, under the greatest pressure imaginable, happened to give Detroit the 1940 pennant.

The pressure on Giebell wasn't just due to the situation in the pennant race on the last weekend of the season. It was also because the 30-year-old rookie, who had been hacking around the minor leagues for years, was matched against the greatest pitcher of the times—Bob Feller.

Giebell was a lanky right-hander who had been up briefly the previous year, pitched relief, split two decisions, and had a decent ERA of 2.93. It wasn't enough to stick, though. Although the Tigers had lagged since winning it all in 1935, their pitching staff was deep. Bobo Newsom was an ace, and two old heroes, Tommy Bridges and Schoolboy Rowe, were still around. After fighting years of arm problems, Rowe was a special surprise, going 16–3 for the season.

NO HITS FOR JUSTIN

There had not been a no-hitter pitched in Detroit by a member of the Tigers for 55 years. Justin Verlander snapped that streak on June 12, 2007. In his second year in the majors, Verlander went out and stifled Milwaukee, one of the best hitting teams in the National League, before a rapturous Comerica Park crowd.

A backhanded grab behind second base by reserve infielder Neifi Perez, who then started a double play, saved the no-no in the eighth inning.

In addition, there was some great young talent in Hal Newhouser, Dizzy Trout, and Fred Hutchinson. There was no room for an aging kid like Giebell. So he went down to the Buffalo farm club—not even compiling a winning record there—but was recalled in September for the last month of the season.

This had been a tight pennant race and a nasty one. The Tigers and Indians not only leapfrogged past each other repeatedly for first place, their fans took it personally. Players were bombarded with garbage on the field and when they arrived in town at the team hotels. Tigers catcher Birdie Tebbetts was knocked cold when one such shower landed on his head in Cleveland.

Fueling much of the antagonism was a player rebellion against Indians manager Ossie Vitt. According to newspaper reports, the Indians were complaining about his strict disciplinary actions. On their next trip into Detroit, the Tigers hung baby clothes in their dugout to taunt the "crybaby Indians."

The Indians had the toughest pitching staff in the league but couldn't match Detroit's down-the-lineup power. Hank Greenberg and Rudy York had driven in 284 runs between them. The Indians also had some good hitters in their lineup, including young stars Lou Boudreau and Kenny Keltner, but nothing like the Tigers' big sticks.

Feller was the great equalizer. He was having his greatest year, winning 27 games and leading the league in strikeouts for the third straight season. At the age of 21 he was unchallenged as the top pitcher in all of baseball, the last man you'd want to see on the mound against you in a big game.

Just two years previously he had set a record by whiffing 18 Tigers. Now he was set to deflate Detroit again in the first game of this deciding series.

Detroit was hot down the stretch, winning nine of its previous 11 games. They were two games in front coming into Cleveland. Just one more win would give them the pennant.

Indians fans had threatened to greet the Tigers with more abuse and rotten vegetables when they disembarked from their train. A few of the players thought about having cabs waiting at the back door of the station. Newsom was having none of that. "I'll leave the way I always do, through the front door," he insisted.

Meanwhile, Tigers manager Del Baker had decided that in some situations, maybe the back door was best. If Feller beat the Tigers, at the worst their lead would be shaved to one game with two to play, and he'd still have two of his top pitchers ready to go.

So he decided on Giebell.

The rookie had started the first game of a doubleheader against the woeful A's the week before and coasted in with a 13–2 win. It wasn't a great test, but he had pitched a complete game.

Giebell had a decent fastball, although nothing close to what Feller threw. His bread-and-butter pitch, however, was a change-up. Baker figured that if the Indians hadn't seen it before—and they had no real reason to have scouted Giebell in advance—it could be enough to baffle them. And if not, well, the Tigers would still be in first place with two to go.

"I don't think any of us had ever heard of him before," said Feller. "I blinked when I saw him come out to warm up. I had no idea who he was."

The Detroit papers called Giebell a "sacrificial lamb." It was an old and honorable baseball tactic, however. Managers such as Connie Mack and John McGraw had deliberately withheld their best pitchers from a World Series opener rather than pit them against the other team's ace.

And if they actually happened to win the game, the psychological advantage would be immense.

Giebell's main problem was control, which had a disturbing tendency to desert him. But on this Friday afternoon he had command of all his pitches.

Feller was at his best, too. But in the fourth, York fisted a two-run homer down the left-field line and the Tigers led 2–0. That was all they would get. It was up to Giebell to make it stand up.

Which he did. For nine innings, the Indians could not figure him out. He shut them out on six hits, and the Tigers won their third pennant in seven years. They lost the final two as the regulars rested, but the race was over.

Giebell never won another game with the Tigers. He was ineligible for the Series and when he came back in 1941, he was wild and ineffective. The Tigers sent him down to Buffalo, and then the war came along and his career as a ballplayer was finished.

Giebell died in 2004 at the age of 94. Family members told reporters that among his most cherished possessions was a silver tray signed by every player on the 1940 Tigers. It was the gift he received in return for giving them the pennant.

THE SOLDIER RETURNS (1945)

You wonder what their career stats might have looked like had the war not taken them away in their prime. Ted Williams, Bob Feller, Joe DiMaggio—all of them missed years that would have enhanced their standings in every category. Feller never won 300, Williams never hit 600 homers. Not that they needed it for Hall of Fame credentials. Still, you wonder.

Maybe the biggest numerical gap was Hank Greenberg's. He was among the first ballplayers to enlist, leaving the Tigers even before Pearl Harbor, just 19 games into the 1941 season. He was 30 years old, acknowledged as the top home-run threat in the game. He had pounded out 249 in just seven full seasons, although he missed almost the entire 1936 campaign with a wrist injury.

When he came back from the war, the question was whether he would be able to pick it up again. He had missed the equivalent of four full midcareer seasons and he wasn't a kid anymore.

One can only wonder what slugger Hank Greenberg's career stats would have been had he not enlisted in the army before Pearl Harbor in 1941. Photo courtesy of Getty Images.

He also was returning to a team in the middle of a pennant race. In addition to all that, the defensively challenged Rudy York was a fixture at first base, and Greenberg would have to take his aging legs into the outfield.

The war had turned everything upside down. With the stars in the military, consistent tailenders, like the St. Louis Browns and the Washington Senators, turned into contenders. Browns president Bill DeWitt sized up the challenge and set about to assemble the deepest pool of 4-Fs in the majors.

They rewarded him with a pennant in 1944, the only one the franchise would ever win. The Tigers lost out by one game. Now, one year later, it was the Senators who had risen from the depths to challenge Detroit.

The Browns had won with just 89 victories the year before, and it was apparent that it might not even take that many this time around. The talent was spread around thinly but evenly, and four teams came into September with a decent chance of winning.

Greenberg had returned in late spring, after the war in Europe ended. The Tigers figured that half a season out of him was as good as a full year out of most of their talent. The power numbers were down all through the league anyhow in this final wartime season, even among established home-run hitters. York could manage just 18 to lead the Tigers, and Vern Stephens topped the league with 24.

So when Greenberg chipped in with 13 homers and 60 RBIs in just 78 games, it was no small addition.

Like most teams of this era, the Tigers were a hodgepodge of has-beens and never-weres. Their sparkplug was second baseman Eddie Mayo, 35 years old and a career minor leaguer—at least until now. Fan favorite Doc Cramer was 40 but still played a serviceable center field. Long ago he had played for Connie Mack in the 1931 World Series, and he longed to get back.

But the core of the team was the pitching combination of Hal Newhouser and Dizzy Trout. Between them they won 43 games, and no other team in the league could match that.

Still, the Senators would not be shaken off. Their home field, Griffith Stadium, was known as a pitcher's paradise, and, because they hit only 27 home runs in the entire year, this team relied almost totally on its pitching. That's 27 home runs for the entire team. The leader was Harlond Clift, who finished with eight homers. Those were dead-ball–era numbers.

On the other hand, their top-two base runners, George Case and George Myatt, stole 60 bases, which was as much as the entire Detroit team. So things balanced out.

The race had one of the strangest endings in history. The Senators had finished their season a week earlier on September 23, with a record of 87–67. They had no games scheduled for the next weekend because the Washington Redskins had prior claim on the use of the field. Wartime travel restrictions were still in effect, although Japan had surrendered in August, and scheduling arrangements were difficult.

The Tigers were one game ahead at 87–65 heading into the last day of the season, September 30. If they won just once more, they would clinch the pennant. Lose two and there would be a playoff. Their season was scheduled to end with two weekend games in St. Louis. But on Saturday it rained, which meant a Sunday doubleheader as a finale. Rain was moving in again, and the Tigers needed to wrap it up and get their rotation ready for the Series.

Newhouser pitched two shutouts down the stretch. But he didn't get the call. Instead, in another quirk of this strange season, the nod went to Virgil Trucks. He was also coming back from the service, and the commissioner's office waived the usual rules, deciding such players would be eligible for the Series even if they had not been on the active roster on September 1. Since Trucks would join the Series rotation, it was important to get him some practice, even if that meant starting him for the first time in two years in a pennant-clinching game. (Stranger still was the story of Cubs catcher Clyde McCullough, who played in the Series without being in a single regular-season game. It's the only time that ever happened.)

Trucks carried a 2–1 lead into the sixth before leaving the game. But the Browns rallied late, and, when the Tigers came to bat in the ninth with the skies darkening, they trailed 3–2.

Detroit put runners on third and second with one out and Cramer coming to the plate. After a hurried consultation, manager

Zack Taylor decided to walk Cramer. The problem with that strategy was that the on-deck hitter was Greenberg.

As Detroit fans clustered by their radios, the hero of seasons past dug in with the bases loaded. In later years Cramer liked to jokingly brag that he was once walked to get to Greenberg. But the Browns were hoping for something on the ground to turn a game-ending double play.

Instead they got something into the left-field pavilion at Sportsman's Park, a grand-slam homer that clinched the pennant. The second game was washed out, but it didn't matter anymore. The soldier had come home and lifted Detroit to another pennant.

In the nine seasons Greenberg spent with the Tigers, the team won four pennants. No other Tiger ever matched that winning proficiency. He then went on to hit .304 in the Series with seven RBIs, while Trucks won Game 2 and threw a complete game.

And with that, the wartime years were finally over.

THE NEW SHORTSTOP [1968]

Mayo Smith did not like to gamble. He was a by-the-book manager with a veteran team. He put his best player at every position and let it happen.

But now he was faced with an unprecedented situation. The face of Detroit baseball for more than a decade, Al Kaline, had finally caught a winner. Yet he was not scheduled to play in the World Series. There was no room in the lineup.

Kaline had gone down in May, when an inside fastball from Oakland's Lew Krausse Jr. shattered his left hand. While he was recovering from the injury, the Detroit outfield of Willie Horton, Jim Northrup, and Mickey Stanley was winning a pennant—a goal Kaline had vainly pursued for years.

Now the team would finally be in the World Series, and Kaline would be on the bench. To a baseball lifer like Smith, this was unthinkable. But what was he supposed to do?

Kaline tried to make it easy for him by going to his office privately in the last few weeks before the postseason and telling him

CASEY'S BIG BAT

Detroit's biggest clutch performance in a World Series was turned in by Sean Casey. Despite the fact that the Tigers lost in five in 2006, Casey went nine for 17 and drove in five of the 11 runs they scored in the entire Series. His .529 average was the highest ever for a Detroit player.

that he understood. Mayo had to do what was best for the team. Smith consulted with general manager Jim Campbell, another great traditionalist who eschewed risk.

There was some talk about playing Kaline at third, a position he had filled in at twice in his career. But that sounded absurd, playing one of the greatest defensive outfielders in the history of the game at such a strange position. Kaline had played many more games at first, but that too was a problem. It would mean benching Norm Cash, and he deserved this shot in the Series almost as much as Kaline.

Everyone on the Tigers knew that shortstop was a problem and that the team had gotten through the season rotating three weak-hitting utility infielders there. But they also knew that next to catching, shortstop was the toughest position on the field. It took range, arm, and hands.

If anyone could handle it, though, it would be Stanley. He was the best athlete on the team, and during infield practice he liked to fool around by taking grounders at short. A light went on in Mayo's head. But did he dare to take a risk that great on the biggest of all stages? And would Stanley, a brilliant center fielder, agree to do it?

The pennant was clinched, and there were nine games to go in the season. Stanley agreed to give it a try as the season ended, and after those games were played, Mayo would make a decision. Stanley handled 25 chances in the nine games and made two errors. After the last game, Mayo still would not commit himself. One of Detroit's daily newspapers carried a story saying Stanley was in at shortstop and the other said he was out.

But he was, indeed, to be the shortstop. And the reality of the situation was hitting home to the 26-year-old Stanley.

"I tried to make everybody think I was calm and in control of everything," he said. "But my insides were churning. Cash said that my ass was so tight, they couldn't have taken a pin out of it with a backhoe."

In Game 2 Stanley made a throwing error on a grounder to deep short. He made a second error on a grounder in Game 6 with the Tigers ahead 13–0. Neither one figured in the scoring. In the pressure-packed Game 7, with the teams deadlocked at 0–0, he also started a double play.

Kaline, meanwhile, hit .379 for the victorious Tigers and drove in eight runs to tie Northrup for the team lead. Mayo's gamble, perhaps the greatest in World Series history, had paid off.

The story, unfortunately, has a melancholy end. Mayo was so enthused by his plan's success that he decided to make Stanley his regular shortstop in 1969. But the throwing motion at that position was far different from what Stanley was accustomed to in the outfield, and he ended up injuring his arm. He returned to his regular job in center, but never again threw with the same strength he had before.

Sparky Anderson pulled his own pressurized switcheroo in the 1984 Series. He named Marty Castillo and Darrell Evans to platoon as his third basemen. Tom Brookens, the regular at the spot, was hiding a hamstring injury and had no range, and Sparky did not trust the defense of Howard Johnson in tough situations.

But it wasn't quite the same. Castillo, normally the backup catcher, had played third base several times in the previous two seasons. Evans had been a regular third baseman for several years with the Braves and the Giants. He was now a first baseman/designated hitter, though, and had only played 19 games at third during the season.

Playing third, however, is not like playing shortstop, and Castillo even punched out a two-run homer in Game 3. So that gamble in the clutch ended happily, too.

NUMBERS DON'T LIE (OR DO THEY?)

SCHOOLBOY'S 16 (1934)

The longest wait between Tigers pennants lasted 25 seasons, from 1909 to 1934. There was a near miss by two and a half games to Boston in 1915. Other than that, Detroit usually finished well down in the standings.

The explanation was fairly clear. The Tigers were known for their batting champs and run producers. There were Hall of Famers up and down their lineup. But the pitching never matched up.

For most of those years, it was Hooks Dauss—the franchise's all-time winner with 221 victories—against the world. In the late '20s Earl Whitehill arrived as a dependable starter. But the Tigers could never put together a staff with depth. That changed in a hurry in 1934.

The arrival of Mickey Cochrane and Goose Goslin and the emergence of Hank Greenberg as a home-run threat are usually given as the big reasons for Detroit's sudden vault from a distant fifth place to a pennant. But just as essential was the fact that Elden Auker and Schoolboy Rowe turned into big-time pitchers. The 1934 Tigers could, at long last, throw out a rotation of four men who won at least 15 games—Auker and Rowe along with veterans Tommy Bridges and Firpo Marberry. For the first time since the dead-ball era, they had two starters with more than 20 wins.

Bridges, who finished at 22–11, had been steadily improving, with two 14-win seasons in a row. But the arrival of Rowe changed

The Detroit Tigers pitching staff with manager Mickey Cochrane. From left: Schoolboy Rowe, Cochrane, Elden Auker, Tommy Bridges, and Alvin Crowder. Rowe and Auker, especially, are credited with making the 1930s Tigers into a winning team.

everything. The 24-year-old fastballer from Arkansas went 24–8 and for most of the season was quite literally unbeatable. Between May and August, Rowe won 16 games in a row to tie an American League record while the Tigers pulled away from the pack.

He had come up from the minors halfway through the 1933 season and showed a good deal of promise, winning seven games. But no one could have expected this.

"He had one of the finest fastballs I ever stood behind," said Charlie Gehringer. "He was so tall, and looking at the ball from second base, I swear it looked like it was going to hit the ground. But they were strikes. That ball would carry in there and it had plenty of smoke on it."

The streak began innocuously enough. The Tigers had lost all four of his early starts, and Rowe was getting cuffed around pretty good. The team had a home game with Boston on May 27. They were in third place, just a couple of games over .500, and weren't raising anyone's pulse rate. Rowe got the start and beat the Red Sox, which was not hard to do in the mid-1930s, outlasting Gordon Rhodes (one of a succession of ballplayers whose nickname inevitably was "Dusty") by a 6–4 score. Then it went on from there.

Rowe was what they used to call "country," just a big old farm boy from cotton country near El Dorado. The Schoolboy nickname, attached to him as a raw kid at spring training, followed him through his entire 15-year career. The other players usually referred to him as "Schoolie." No one ever used his given name of Lynwood.

By midsummer, Rowe and the Tigers had become a national story. After his first win, the team went on an 83–37 tear, and Rowe was mowing down anyone who stood in the way. He came in and pitched relief a few times and won six games that way, too. In July he beat the Yankees twice in a four-game series at Navin Field, and the Tigers swept past New York into the league lead. He had then won 10 in a row.

The pitching sensation was interviewed on a national radio hookup after that performance. Just as the program closed, he couldn't resist sending a message to his fiancée back home. "How'm I doin', Edna?" he said.

The bench jockeys never let it go. Every time he walked to the mound, they'd call out from the other dugout in a chirping falsetto, "How'm I doin', Edna?" But Schoolie was unfazed. The caravan rolled on.

August came, and the Tigers kept widening their lead. Rowe duplicated his earlier feat against the Yankees, beating them twice in four games at Yankee Stadium and shutting them out in the finale. His streak went to 13 in a row, then 14 and 15.

He was now going after a record held by three of the league's legendary pitchers—Walter Johnson, Smoky Joe Wood, and Lefty Grove. The entire city was caught up in the drama, and his teammates knew that they were seeing history. Even the major league record, Rube Marquard's 19 in a row, didn't seem beyond Rowe's reach. Mickey Cochrane, perhaps not incidentally, was the catcher for both Grove and Rowe.

On August 25 the Tigers arrived in Washington, and Rowe was matched against Monte Weaver. Schoolie was going for the league record on Johnson's home field, and not many in that crowd were pulling for him.

"We knew how much he wanted that record and we were breaking our backs for him," recalled Gehringer. "We were behind 2–1 in the ninth. Then we put two men on, and Greenberg brought them in with a double. So Rowe had his 16th in a row."

The streak ended the very next time out. Philadelphia bombed him, 13–5. Even so, Rowe won eight more times that year. When he shut out the Yankees for a second time on September 18, Detroit's lead had grown to seven and a half games. No one was going to catch them now.

Rowe won once more in the World Series. He also finished the year hitting .303 with 11 of his 33 hits going for extra bases. There was very little that Schoolie could do wrong in 1934.

He would win 19 games in each of the next two seasons, too, before his arm went dead. Still, he managed to reinvent himself as a control artist and went 16–3 for the 1940 pennant winners before ending his career in the National League.

But for 94 days during the summer of 1934, there was no better pitcher in baseball.

THE MOOSE AND LITTLE CESAR (1952, 1970)

Their careers with the Tigers may have been brief, but Walt Dropo and Cesar Gutierrez stuck around long enough to establish two records for consecutive hits.

This is one time the numbers really don't tell the story, though, because both players were disappointments in Detroit.

MR. CONSISTENT

They called Charlie Gehringer "the Mechanical Man" because his consistency was almost timed to a Swiss movement. Lefty Gomez made the famous wisecrack, "You wind Gehringer up on Opening Day and he hits .333, and at the end of the season he's still hitting .333."

Well, not quite. Actually his lifetime average was .320. His batting average for the 20 World Series games he was in? It was .321, of course.

Carl Hubbell's feat of striking out five of the American League's top sluggers in a row in the 1933 All-Star Game is still celebrated. What is less well-remembered is that Gehringer preceded all of that with a single. He also played four seasons in which he came to bat more than 600 times and struck out fewer than 20 of them.

Those numbers don't lie.

Dropo's performance came first. He was a 6'5" first baseman who came from the town of Moosup, Connecticut. Naturally, he was nicknamed Moose. He was a high school and college football star and received offers from the NFL to come and play in its yard.

He broke into the majors in 1950 with Boston instead, in one of the most spectacular rookie seasons on record. Dropo hit .322 with 34 homers and a league-leading 144 RBIs. The Sox looked set at that position for years.

But in 1951 Dropo broke his wrist, and although he played another 10 years, he was never the same power hitter. Still, when he was offered to the Tigers as part of a blockbuster deal that sent George Kell to Boston in 1952, Detroit decided to take a chance.

The trade was done in early June when it was clear that the Tigers, pennant contenders only two years before, were old and tired and headed for the basement. This was the first last-place finish in franchise history and a sad, strange trip it was.

Dropo inherited the first-base job by default and turned in a credible job. Then one afternoon in mid-July he suddenly caught fire at Yankee Stadium. After being pummeled 11–1 and 12–2 in a doubleheader, the Tigers rose up and smote one of New York's second line pitchers, Jim McDonald, 8–2.

Dropo went five for five. Tellingly, all of his hits were singles.

The Tigers dragged themselves on to Washington, where their pitchers were subjected to further brutalization. The Nats bombed them 8–2 and 9–8 in another doubleheader. But Dropo rolled merrily along.

He went seven for seven in the two games, including a home run. After making an out, he then got three more hits. The 12 consecutive hits in 12 times at bat tied the record, and his 15 hits in three games set another one. For two dizzying days, it appeared that the old Dropo was back.

But not for long. No one could continue at that pace, of course, but Dropo dropped off to a rather ordinary .276 for the season. The following year he dipped another 28 points, and in 1955 he departed for the White Sox, leaving his record behind as a souvenir.

Oddly enough, the record he tied was established by Pinky Higgins in 1938. Like Dropo, he also was traded from Boston to Detroit. But he got his 12 hits in a row right before the deal was made instead of right after. Sometimes there is a pattern to these things.

Gutierrez was at the other end of the physical scale from Dropo. The shortstop from Venezuela was only 5'9", and his nickname, Cocoa, seemed to reflect his diminutive stature.

The Tigers were constantly seeking a shortstop in the late '60s, especially one who could hit a little. They had won a pennant in 1968 rotating three players at the position, none of whom hit more than .203. Ray Oyler, in fact, went hitless for the last two months of the season. So when Gutierrez became available late the following year, it seemed worth a shot.

He'd been given two very brief trials with the Giants, but in 17 games with the Tigers he hit .245. In the Detroit scheme of things, that constituted a major improvement. So when the 1970 season began, he got the starting job.

By mid-June, however, things were not going so well. The team was sagging in the race, and Gutierrez was giving them nothing offensively. He also made a lot of errors.

The Tigers had a Father's Day doubleheader in Cleveland, and he sat out the first game, which Detroit won 7–2. Manager Mayo Smith decided to bat him number two in the second game. He singled to right his first time up, but that seemed fairly irrelevant as the Indians jumped on starter Mike Kilkenny for five runs before he could get out of the first inning. By the time Gutierrez came up again, it was 6–1.

Gutierrez singled again, and this time Al Kaline stroked one out of the park. That closed the gap to 6–3. Then Gutierrez beat out a hit to deep shortstop in the fifth for his third straight hit. By then it was 6–5 and things were getting interesting. Fathers were awakening from their holiday naps all over Detroit and tuning in on the radio.

Next time up, Gutierrez varied the scenario and doubled. Cleveland had widened its lead to 8–5 by then, but when he rode home on Jim Northrup's homer, it was a one-run game again. Cesar took care of that at the earliest opportunity, slashing out his fifth straight hit in the eighth, a single that drove in the tying run.

That also was his ticket into the record books. Because if the game had ended in a nine-inning Cleveland win, he would have finished with a five-for-five afternoon. Excellent, but not extraordinary. He reached that next level in extra innings.

In the tenth he legged out yet another hit to deep shortstop. That made six in a row. But he wasn't done yet. When he came to bat again in the twelfth, Mickey Stanley, hitting ahead of him in the lineup, had just homered, giving Detroit a 9–8 lead. Gutierrez then whipped out his seventh consecutive hit, a sharp single to center.

And for the icing on the cake, he then set out to steal second. Unfortunately, he was thrown out by several feet. Not that it mattered. The Tigers won, and Gutierrez's seven hits in one game without an out established the record.

His average shot up 31 points in that one day. It was nothing to get excited about, though. He finished the year at .243, and if you deducted the results of that one game, it was 13 points lower than that.

The next year he played in only 38 games and then was cut, never to play in the majors again. How many hits did he get in those final 38 games? Exactly seven.

NO-NO TIMES TWO (1952)

By any standard you care to name, 5–19 is a pretty rotten season. Especially for a pitcher who was regarded as one of the elite starters in the American League.

Virgil Trucks won a World Series game, led the league in strikeouts and shutouts one season, and had a career mark of 103–72. He was 35, still at the top of his form, and the Tigers expected another big year from him in 1952.

Instead, the season featured a complete collapse of the team that had nearly won a pennant only two years before. The Tigers lost their first eight games, scoring a grand total of 14 runs in the process. Still, ballclubs do go into slumps, and there was every reason to believe these veterans could get themselves straightened out.

But it never happened, and in June the Tigers began to blow up the team. George Kell, Hoot Evers, Dizzy Trout, Johnny Lipon—all of them gone in one fell swoop in a June trade with Boston. A month later, Fred Hutchinson was released, and in August Vic Wertz joined the exodus.

The Tigers would finish so far in the basement that sunlight could not penetrate. They were last in pitching, last in runs, and at 50–104 the Tigers were last in the standings for the first time ever. Trucks, who had spent his entire career in Detroit, found himself sharing the clubhouse with strangers.

It was an odd trip down, though. Walt Dropo, as noted above, tied the record for consecutive hits that season with 12. Art Houtteman broke the season-opening losing streak by taking a no-hitter into the ninth before finally giving up a two-out single to Cleveland's Suitcase Simpson.

By May 15 the team was 7–18 and had lost every game Trucks started. He was scheduled to pitch against Washington and Bob Porterfield that afternoon before a dedicated group of paying customers at Briggs Stadium. Only 2,215 were in the stands, while a much larger crowd was lining the streets of downtown for a parade to honor General Douglas MacArthur.

The Senators weren't all that much better, either, that year. They were the only team in the league that hit worse than the Tigers. But they did have legitimate threats in their lineup. Mickey Vernon and Pete Runnels would each become two-time batting champs, and Jackie Jensen went on to a fine career in Boston. Porterfield was also their best pitcher, a 13-game winner that season.

As it turned out, both starters were in rare form. One inning followed another, and the game remained scoreless. By the seventh, Trucks had not yet given up a hit, and the Tigers had managed just three off Porterfield.

Virgil Trucks holds up a ball in the clubhouse after throwing his no-hitter on August 25, 1952.

Trucks was accomplishing this while pitching in borrowed shoes. His feet were swollen, and he couldn't get into his own spikes. Houtteman, who had come so close to a no-hitter, offered his slightly larger pair. Apparently there was a little bit of magic remaining in them. Like Houtteman one month before, Trucks entered the ninth still holding on to his no-hitter.

He had lost a nine-inning no-hitter in the minors when the game went into the tenth. As the first two Tigers went down in the ninth, he started thinking about that game again. Next up was Wertz, who had doubled off Porterfield earlier only to get himself picked off second. He had been Detroit's top home-run hitter for several seasons, topping out at 27 the previous two years. The short right field at the ballpark was made for him.

Wertz swung at the first pitch and smashed it off the overhanging second deck. Trucks leaped to his feet and banged his head on the dugout roof, leaving him dazed and bewildered when he ran out to greet Wertz at the plate. But he had his no-hitter.

It didn't stop the downward spiral for the Tigers, though. In late August, when they went into New York to meet the first-place Yankees, they were 40 games below .500. Not only did they trail the Yanks by 30 games, they were eight and a half behind the seventh-place St. Louis Browns.

It was Trucks's turn to start on August 27. Only two Tigers who had been in the lineup for his classic in May—Johnny Groth and Steve Souchock—were still around by this time. It was pretty much a different team. But the Yankees were very much the Yankees, on the way to winning their fourth straight championship.

Mickey Mantle was in their lineup and so were fellow Hall of Famers Yogi Berra and Phil Rizzuto. Trucks drew one of the lesser New York starters, rookie Bill Miller. He had won only four games that year and wouldn't even get into the World Series. After all, why waste one of your top guns on the Tigers? On this day, though, he was up to the task.

But in the seventh, the Tigers finally broke through for a run on a double by Dropo and a Souchock single. The real suspense, however, came on an official scorer's ruling back in the third.

Rizzuto had bounced one to shortstop Johnny Pesky, who seemed to have a problem getting the ball out of his glove. His throw was late, and scorer John Drebinger, the highly respected baseball writer for the *New York Times*, ruled it an error.

Then he began having second thoughts. Could Pesky have made the play even if he had fielded it cleanly? He changed his decision to a hit. But as the innings rolled on and Trucks still had not given up another hit, Drebinger was conflicted. By the seventh inning, other writers were urging him to call the Detroit dugout and check with Pesky, a rather unusual move. Pesky dutifully told him that it was a ball he should have handled, and Drebinger changed it back to an error.

Even the Yankee Stadium crowd cheered when the ruling went up on the scoreboard. But Trucks still had three innings to get through, and the matter of Yankees pride was at stake.

One of their own, Allie Reynolds, had pitched two no-hitters just the previous year, tying the mark set by Johnny Vander Meer in 1938—although his came on successive starts. So the Yankees had an added incentive to break up this one against Trucks.

But Mantle started the ninth by striking out, and then Joe Collins hit a fly ball to center. That left it up to Hank Bauer, who sent a hard grounder to second base. The play was made routinely, and Trucks had his second no-hitter of this otherwise dismal year.

After the season, the Tigers sent him on his way. He went to the Browns, who mercifully passed him on to a good White Sox team. In the next two seasons he won 20 and 19 games for them.

He still had plenty of stuff left in his right arm. The two no-hitters had proven that. It was the 5–19 record that was the lie.

LORD OF THE TRIPLE [1903–1916]

If there is one Tigers statistic that appears to be a permanently secure record, it is the 309 career triples of Sam Crawford.

Once upon a time, the three-base hit was the gold standard for power hitters. While home-run titles could be won with single digits, it took more than 20 triples to get that distinction. No one

Sam Crawford had an astonishing 312 career triples for the Tigers during an era when they seemed to matter more than home runs.
Photo courtesy of Getty Images.

spoke about a triple crown—batting average, RBIs, and homers. In the dead-ball era, it was the triple champ who wore the crown.

Crawford led the league in triples six times in his career. In fact, the only one close to him in triples production was his teammate, Ty Cobb, who did it four times and finished just 14 career triples behind Crawford.

It is no wonder they were the most feared hitting combination of their time, as formidable as Babe Ruth and Lou Gehrig were in their era. Still, it's hard for contemporary fans, attuned to the home run as the true measure of the long ball, to understand what a force they were.

After all, triples don't make it on *SportsCenter* at ESPN. Going yard does.

It remains one of the most exciting plays in the game, requiring a blend of power and speed. The big guys stop at second when they drive one deep into the gap or into the corners. Only the quickest make it to third.

In Crawford's era, the home run was regarded as somewhat less than manly. All it took was brawn and a slow trot, although it should be pointed out that Crawford led the league three times in that department, too. While still playing for Cincinnati, he hit 16 homers in 1901. No one in the National League would reach that figure for the next 10 years.

Veteran Detroit sportswriter H.G. Salsinger once wrote that he clearly recalled outfielders pulling in some of Crawford's drives with their backs against the wall—"balls that surely would have been home runs when the live ball came in."

Signing Crawford is what gave the Tigers credibility, much as the signing of free agent Pudge Rodriguez would do more than a century later. The two-year-old team was bereft of big-name stars when it persuaded Crawford to jump from the National League.

He arrived in 1903 and promptly hit 25 triples to lead the league, naturally. But it wasn't until the arrival of Cobb a few years later that Crawford developed into one of the league's superstars. In fact, in the intervening two seasons before Cobb showed up, he never hit .300.

But with Crawford hitting third in the batting order, right in front of Cobb, no one was going to pitch around him. In some years they reversed those positions, but with that sort of protection in the lineup, Crawford rarely dropped below .300 again and led the league in RBIs three times.

It goes without saying, however, that, along with just about everybody else on the Tigers team, he hated Cobb. The two barely spoke for years, although Crawford said they devised a set of hand signals.

In years when Cobb batted third, he would frequently end up on third, either through a triple or by stealing a base or two. The rattled pitcher might then walk Crawford.

"I'd sort of half glance at Cobb on third," he said. "He'd make a slight move that told me he wanted me to keep going and not stop at first. Well, I'd trot down the line and then, suddenly, without warning, I'd speed up and go as fast as I could and tear out for second. They're watching him on third, and there I go, and they don't know what the devil to do."

Crawford's ability to hit Walter Johnson, one of the rare pitchers who could handle Cobb, also infuriated Ty. What Cobb didn't know was that Johnson was fond of Crawford's bats. Whenever Crawford let him use one, he would ease up on him. Crawford would get a hit and Cobb would fume, unable to understand how Crawford was able to get to Johnson so often.

Baseball was also a regional game in those years, and there were relatively few players on the Tigers (besides Cobb) who came from the South. In those days before extensive scouting systems and the free-agent draft, teams tended to concentrate on talent from their own backyards.

So the Tigers were well stocked with ballplayers from the Midwest and, in the words of Nebraskan Crawford, "Ty always seemed as if he was refighting the Civil War."

In later life, Cobb insisted that Crawford would deliberately foul off pitches if it appeared that he had a base stolen. The two never patched things up.

Nonetheless, the men combined to give the Tigers three straight pennants, a streak the team has never equaled. They lost all three World Series, though, mostly because both of them proved to be duds in that showcase. Cobb hit .267—almost exactly 100 points below his lifetime average—and Crawford hit only .243.

The years go by, and Crawford's name is probably unfamiliar to most Detroit fans today. There is no statue of him in the center-field pavilion at Comerica Park, and since he played in an era before uniforms had numbers, his couldn't very well be retired. He also left Detroit right after his career ended and seldom returned, spending most of the remainder of his life in California.

Still, most of the records that Cobb once held have fallen, even those for career hits and stolen bases that were regarded as unassailable. But Crawford's triples stand alone.

30 FOR DENNY (1968)

At times it seemed the entire 1968 season was simply intended as a backdrop for Denny McLain. His pursuit of one of baseball's magic stats loomed larger and larger as the season progressed.

Sure, the Tigers were winning the pennant, and that was great. But by late summer it was also a foregone conclusion. McLain's attempt to become the first pitcher in 34 years to reach 30 wins became the biggest sports story in America. Even the other Tigers, including those who did not care at all for their brash star, were caught up in it. Everyone likes to be a part of history. So as the season rolled into September, McLain's race eclipsed everything else.

Number 27 came on the first of the month against the Orioles. Denny even started a triple play on a line drive hit back to him to keep the customers amused. He said if it hadn't caught it, the ball would have smashed him in the face. Photographs showed he caught it around his belt.

The Twins provided victim number 28 five days later, and then the show rolled on to southern California, the epicenter of media hype. There were almost as many showbiz celebrities in the clubhouse and reporters in the press box as people in the stands as Denny stopped the Angels 7–2. Now all was in readiness for the grand finale.

It was scheduled to happen on a Saturday afternoon against Oakland at Tiger Stadium. It was more like a run-up to a coronation than a ballgame. Dizzy Dean, the last man to win 30, showed up (and was denied access to the press box by the Detroit chapter president of the Baseball Writers' Association, whose own newspaper had hired Dean to write about the event). Sandy Koufax, who was the last man to hold the title of Greatest Pitcher in America, was covering for NBC, the national TV network.

When the season began, this date had looked like a dead spot on the schedule. So to fill the house the Tigers had donated thousands of seats in the left-field grandstands to safety patrol kids from Detroit and the suburbs. The paid attendance was just 33,000, but thousands more were there as freebies and their youthful voices added a strange shrill note to the day's proceedings.

The A's were determined not to be the stooges in this show. This was the team that would dominate the American League in a few more years. Many of those players were already there, including Bert Campaneris, Sal Bando, Catfish Hunter, and a 22-year-old Reggie Jackson. But it wasn't their time. Not yet.

YORK'S HOT AUGUST

One of the more enduring Tigers records was Rudy York's mark of blasting 18 home runs in one month, during August 1937. A defensively challenged third baseman, York had just been moved to catcher, replacing injured player/manager Mickey Cochrane, when he went on his tear.

Fittingly enough, when the Cubs' Sammy Sosa broke York's mark 61 years later, his 19th homer of the month was blasted into the right-field seats at Tiger Stadium.

As they took batting practice, one of the A's walked around with a sign on his neck that read: "Dobson goes for number 12 today." Chuck Dobson had drawn the assignment against McLain, and for his Oakland teammates it was almost like a World Series game.

This was a time when umpires tended to give pitchers the high strike, and McLain was most effective working high in the strike zone. He gave up lots of home runs that way, but he could also overpower most hitters in that area.

Jackson caught up to him in the fourth with a runner aboard, though, and the A's were off to a 2–0 lead. That didn't last long. Norm Cash crashed a three-run homer in Detroit's half of the inning to put Denny in front 3–2.

Dobson was taken out of the game and two relief pitchers came in to get Oakland out of the inning. The A's may have been a sixth-place team, but their manager, Bob Kennedy, was playing it to the hilt. Then on a walk, a bunt, and a single by Campaneris, Oakland was right back in it, 3–3, in the fifth.

It looked like a struggle for Denny on this day. He usually allowed fewer than two runs a game, and the A's already had three. But this was the season that saw his transformation into a complete pitcher. He knew how to fight his way out of dark places when he was less than brilliant by pitching against hitter expectations. Nonetheless, in the sixth Jackson homered again, a dart into the right-field upper deck. Now it was 4–3, and that's how it stayed into the ninth inning.

McLain settled in grimly, allowing the A's just one more base runner. By the time he finished the ninth, he also had 10 strikeouts. But he was behind by a run and coming out of the game. He was scheduled to lead off the home half of the inning, but it was pinch-hitter Al Kaline who walked to the plate.

Reliever Diego Segui was working his fifth inning, and he had baffled the Tigers. But he had pitched in short relief all year, and five innings was a very long stint for him. Still, Kennedy kept him in the game.

He walked Kaline, but then got Dick McAuliffe on a pop-up and the crowd groaned—it was a high-pitched groan, thanks to the kids in left field, but a groan nonetheless. They were going to get cheated out of witnessing a landmark. But Mickey Stanley singled, and Kaline raced to third with the tying run. Kennedy brought his infield in to choke off the score. The strategy seemed to work when Jim Northrup sent a bouncer right at Danny Cater.

Cater was the top defensive first baseman in the league. He had made only four errors all year. This was the fifth. He threw wild to the plate. Kaline slid home safely and Stanley raced to third with the winning run. The tumult was deafening. Kennedy pulled both his infield and outfield in, and Willie Horton sent a fly ball to medium-deep left. It would have scored Stanley easily even if Jim Gosger had been playing in his normal position. But stationed where he was, the ball cleared his head for a hit.

Denny had won, and so had the Tigers. The cover of *Sports Illustrated* the next week showed him bursting from the Detroit dugout with Kaline's arm draped around his shoulders.

The crowd refused to go home until he came out for a curtain call that took him on a complete circuit of the field.

"I'm just proud to know that man," said Horton in the packed, ecstatic clubhouse, while Koufax simply shook his head and kept murmuring, "Isn't this amazing?"

McLain had set a mark that probably will never be reached again in an era of seven-inning starters, set-up pitchers, closers, and a huge cast of lesser functionaries in every bullpen. He pitched 28 complete games in his 41 starts that year and often said, "If I get into the eighth with a lead, they're going to have to drag me out of the ballgame."

Even with all that, however, McLain wasn't finished. The pennant was clinched a few days later, and the last games of the season were just for practice. Five days after that happy event, it was Denny's turn again. He was facing the Yankees, and everyone knew it was going to be Mickey Mantle's last game in Detroit. The aging slugger was an old 36. He was now just a .237 hitter and home runs came hard. The small crowd gave him a standing ovation as a final tribute when he came to bat in the eighth and so did the Tigers, led by Kaline, in their dugout.

Mantle was tied with Jimmie Foxx at 534 career homers, which was then the third-most in major league history. Denny decided Mantle should have that position all to himself. With the Tigers leading 6–1, he indicated that he would groove a fastball to Mantle. Not quite believing what he had seen, Mantle swung late and fouled it off.

McLain motioned again, and Mantle gave a slight hand signal as to where he wanted it. Denny served it up, and Mantle put it out. There were only 9,000 people in the stands to see it, but the incident was a fitting footnote to McLain's fantastic 31–5 season. And those numbers still shine.

FIELDER'S 51 (1990)

Cecil Fielder was a surprise gift from the mysterious East. He arrived in Detroit in 1990 after spending a season in Japan, a free-agent signing that attracted almost no attention when it was announced a month before spring training.

Fielder had played parts of four seasons in Toronto, and while he occasionally showed some power, it was not enough for the Jays to give him a regular job. So he headed across the Pacific and spent the 1989 season there. He returned transformed.

He was just 26 years old and a brawny 6'3". Besides, the team had nothing to lose. The Tigers had finished dead last in their division and were falling fearfully short in home-run power. Lou Whitaker led the team with 28 and had spent most of his career as a leadoff man. First base, where power hitters traditionally set up shop, was handled by committee, and none of them were big hitters.

So bringing in Fielder to play the position was not much of a gamble, but it paid some of the biggest dividends in franchise history. Fielder became the first member of the Tigers since Hank Greenberg to hit more than 50 home runs in a season—and this was when 50 was still the measure of an elite power hitter. The steroid mess had yet to rear its ugly head, and such numbers were attained without artificial bodily enhancement.

Fielder wasn't too quick, and no one would mistake him for Fred Astaire around the bag. But when baseballs starting flying out of the park, no one seemed to mind. In fact, when he came to bat, it was as if everyone else in the stadium disappeared. The raw power of his swing and the distances his home runs traveled riveted everyone's attention. Sure, he struck out 182 times. But even those events were awesome. His blasts were bound for the upper deck almost every time.

Since Greenberg's 58 homers in 1938, only one Tiger had hit as many as 45. That was Rocky Colavito in 1961. Greenberg also cleared 40 twice more and so had Norm Cash and Darrell Evans.

Al Kaline had never done it. Nor had Rudy York or Willie Horton or Kirk Gibson, big hitters all. So Fielder's quest for 50 became a major story in Detroit. The Tigers were also improved, not yet a .500 team, to be sure, but finishing just nine games out of first in the Eastern Division. Compared to 1989, a team so bad that it drove manager Sparky Anderson to leave town for a couple of weeks, that was a major improvement.

Fielder was a big part of the step up. He drove in 132 runs, also the most in one year since Colavito, and hit three homers in one game twice during the season.

By September the Tigers were clearly out of the pennant race, but Fielder was deeply involved in his own quest. He got number 49 on September 27, and with six games left in the season, it looked like a cinch. But the entire team suddenly went cold. In the next five games they scored a total of only seven runs, and none of them was a Fielder production.

The Twins stopped him in three games at Tiger Stadium and then it was on to Yankee Stadium, hardly the friendliest park for right-handed hitters, to end the season.

This was a period in which the Yankees were in a stupor. They hadn't been to the World Series in nine years, and George Steinbrenner was raging and firing managers right and left. There weren't any big names going out to stop Fielder.

In the opener, it was Chuck Cary, a former Tiger. While Frank Tanana and two relievers blanked the Yanks on three hits, Fielder took the collar in four at-bats. Then it was Mark Leiter's turn to pitch. Sparky had moved Fielder up to the second slot in the batting order to give him more swings, to no avail. Again he was zero for four.

Just one more chance, and as luck would have it the Yankees pitcher was Steve Adkins, a wild, rookie left-hander. This seemed to set up well. But Adkins was a little too wild. In the first he walked Fielder and then walked the bases loaded. Gary Ward was the one who got the homer, a grand slam. It was his ninth of the year, which was very nice, but 41 short of what Tigers fans wanted to see.

Adkins was still around in the fourth and still fighting for control. He walked Tony Phillips in front of Fielder. And then the suspense ended. Number 50 was a towering drive deep into the left-field seats. It was a fitting end to the quest.

But Fielder wasn't finished. On his last at-bat of the season, with another rookie, Alan Mills, on the mound, Fielder made it 51—the perfect punctuation to an astonishing year.

That big season made Fielder the gate attraction the Tigers had lacked for many years. He followed it up with another great year in 1991, hitting 44 homers and driving in 133 runs. But in the world of contemporary baseball economics, those seasons were a double-edged sword for the Tigers.

The team was sold to Mike Ilitch during the 1992 season, and Fielder's contract expired at its conclusion. His numbers had slipped a little. But still, 35 homers and 124 RBIs were nothing to wave off. Ilitch had pledged to make the Tigers a contender again, and if he wanted to maintain credibility with the fans, that meant he had to re-sign Fielder.

A CLOSER WITH HEART

No player is asked to perform in the clutch more often than a closer. But to John Hiller, who established the Tigers record with 38 saves, that kind of pressure was nothing.

After suffering a heart attack at the age of 27, his career was declared over. But he refused to accept the medical verdict, and worked his way back into shape and back to the Tigers within two years. He was called in to save so many games in 1973 that Billy Martin ordered him to stay away from the park at one stretch and not answer the phone in his hotel so he wouldn't be tempted to call him in again.

His saves record was surpassed by Todd Jones in 2000, but never his courage.

But the team was not getting any better, attendance was stagnant, and a big contract for Fielder meant the Tigers would be strapped in trying to sign free agents. Their top pitcher, David Wells, and number two slugger, catcher Mickey Tettleton, also were cut loose in an effort to reduce expenses.

Fielder himself was finally dealt to the Yankees late in the 1996 season and helped them win their first championship in 18 years—an eternity as New York measures time.

But in less than seven seasons in Detroit he had hit 245 home runs, and that was good for fifth place on the all-time Tigers list.

IT AIN'T OVER 'TIL IT'S OVER

THE FIRST GREAT RALLY (1901)

No one knew whether the Detroit Tigers would last. They didn't even know whether the American League would last.

It was April 25, 1901, and Major League Baseball was returning to Detroit after 13 years. The city had lost its National League franchise after the 1888 season, just one year after winning its only pennant. But now this new entity, which had just declared itself a major league and planned to compete with the old established Nationals, was in business.

Detroit was regarded as a weak link. Bennett Park was a fairly new facility, but it seated just 8,500 people, the smallest in the majors. Many club owners wanted to move the franchise to Pittsburgh. But it was decided to give the city a chance.

This was Detroit's 200th birthday year, and it was not yet the automotive giant that would remake American industry. That was still a few years away. They made stoves and railroad carriages there, and it was notable for its gracious residential streets.

Its new ballclub was an imponderable. They were first named the Tigers in 1895 when the city's team played in the Western League, the precursor to the American League. Like the other new franchises, the Tigers had raided the established teams for talent. They came away with very little.

Several future Hall of Famers jumped from one league to the other. Cy Young, Nap Lajoie, Jimmy Collins, Iron Man Joe

The 1903 Tigers in a photo collage by *Sporting Life*. Ed Barrow, manager, is at center; Sam Crawford, bottom right, was the star of the team. Photo courtesy of Getty Images.

McGinnity—they all made the leap, leaving broken contracts and threats of legal action in their wake. But it stirred up the fans in those cities.

The Tigers, however, got none of the big names. Their first starting lineup would be unfamiliar even to ardent baseball fans today. A few might recognize second baseman Kid Gleason, who would go on to manage the infamous Black Sox of the 1919 World Series. Only pitcher Ed Siever would still be on the roster of the team's first pennant winner, six years in the future. But even he spent a couple of seasons with the St. Louis Browns in between.

So no one knew what to expect from this team in this brave new adventure. It was all unexplored territory. Fortunately, their Opening Day opponent was Milwaukee, whose manager and center fielder was Hugh Duffy, a star on the downside of a great career in Boston. After him there wasn't much, and on the pitching staff there was even less. Their top two pitchers would both lose 20 games, and the team would finish dead last.

A brass band led a parade across the diamond to start things off on this gala Opening Day. It was an overflow crowd, eager to welcome big-time baseball back to town. They filled the stands and a few thousand more stood behind ropes in the outfield. They couldn't have been happy about what they saw.

Roscoe Miller, another of the team's no-names, was given the honor of starting and manager George Stallings must have regretted that quickly. By the third inning, Milwaukee was ahead 7–3, and it kept getting worse.

Pink Hawley, who had once been a pretty good pitcher in the National League and was signed away from the Giants, held the Tigers in check. By the ninth inning he had a 13–4 lead to work

KALINE'S GOOD-BYE

If ever the final few games of a big-league career reflected a player's personality, it was Al Kaline's farewell. His 1974 season was dedicated to two ends: getting 3,000 hits and leaving the stage. Fittingly enough, he reached the first goal in late September in his hometown of Baltimore with a double to left off Dave McNally. The small crowd that had come to see the first-place Orioles applauded warmly.

He left for good eight days later in Detroit. A tiny closing day gathering of around 4,500 hoped to give him a proper salute on his last time at bat. But after flying out to left field as the designated hitter in the third, Kaline asked to come out of the game. Forever.

It was his 2,834th game as a Tiger, the most ever. But Kaline could do without tributes. It was the man's style. No fuss—just simple excellence.

with. Most of the customers had left in disgust. It was going to be a pretty sad return for Detroit.

Even when Doc Casey led off on the Tigers' ninth with a double, there was barely a yawn. Jimmy Barrett singled him home, and then Detroit was nine runs behind. So what? But the hits just kept on coming. Ducky Holmes and Pop Dillon (who was all of 27 years old, despite his nickname) followed with doubles. Fans who were leaving decided to stay a little longer.

Milwaukee couldn't shut the rally down. The Tigers batted around, and when Dillon came up again, the bases were loaded and the score was 13–12 with two outs. Now the fans were screaming. They were seeing one of the most unlikely comebacks they'd ever witnessed.

Dillon didn't let them down. He drove in two runs with a single, and the Tigers had won the game. A 10-run rally in the bottom of the ninth—what a way to start a season, let alone an existence.

Detroit went on to sweep the four-game series, coming back again on Sunday from an 11–5 deficit to score seven runs in the last two innings. The momentum carried the team into the middle of May, when they held on to first place. But it didn't last. Both Chicago and Boston passed them by in the standings, and the Tigers settled back to finish third, eight and a half games off the lead.

Milwaukee was so discouraged that the team moved to St. Louis the next season and became the Browns, which may not come under the heading of progress. Casey, who started off the big rally, became one of the most popular players in Detroit. After his retirement he opened a downtown pharmacy that was a local landmark until his death in 1936.

The first great Tigers rally didn't clinch Detroit's place in the new scheme of baseball. But it gave their fans something to dream about, which was just as good.

THE LAST GREAT RALLY [1999]

Little Bennett Park had grown up. It became Navin Field, then Briggs Stadium, and finally Tiger Stadium. At its peak, after it had been double decked all the way around in 1938, the ballpark could accommodate 54,000 fans for a big night game with the Yankees or a Sunday doubleheader.

Then it started to shrink. Obstructed-view seats were phased out, third-deck tickets and lower-deck bleachers in the center were hardly ever sold. At the end, its capacity was barely 45,000. But as the 1990s wore on and the Tigers explored ever deeper levels of mediocrity, that was no problem. Aside from Opening Day, there was rarely a big demand for tickets.

On a late-September afternoon in 1999, though, the fans came trouping back for one final look, one last afternoon at the corner of Michigan and Trumbull.

The franchise that started its life as a weakling had turned into one of the proudest organizations in the game. There had been nine World Series played on these grounds. The footprints of dozens of Hall of Famers were planted in its turf.

The announced crowd for the final game was something more than 43,000. But there were many more than that, if you counted ghosts. Because everyone in the ballpark carried with them the memory of someone they had loved who had shared a day at this place with them. And they had to be watching, too; waiting for one more bit of excitement, one more thrill, one more late and memorable rally.

And they got it.

The game itself wasn't supposed to be much of an attraction—two subpar .500 teams, the Tigers and Kansas City, playing out the end of a futile season. But it was a chance to say good-bye to all the great players from the past who would come out for a farewell salute when the ballgame ended. That was the draw.

Still, there was a game to be played. Besides, these were supposed to be the stars of the future, the prospects who were finally arriving in the big leagues, those who would bring a flag to Comerica Park in the new century: outfielders Gabe Kapler and Juan Encarnacion, the slugging first baseman Tony Clark, pitchers Jeff Weaver and Brian Moehler. They'd also brought up a young catcher, Robert Fick, who was known as a power hitter.

The fans had selected an all-time Tigers team, and the current players wore those names on the backs of their uniforms as they went out to their positions. Talk about ghosts! Ty Cobb, Charlie Gehringer, and Hank Greenberg were all on the field again—or at least their names were.

Moehler had the honor of starting for this band of immortals, with the name Hal Newhouser on his back. He did it justice, too, holding the Royals to two runs into the seventh.

Luis Polonia delighted the crowd by leading off the first inning with a homer, and Fick drove in another run with a sacrifice fly. The Royals came back to tie it, but when Karim Garcia slammed a two-run shot in the sixth, the lead was 4–2.

But the Tigers were the sort of team with which no lead was safe. Their bullpen could blow one of any size at any time. That's why they were 30 games out of first place.

So when Royals rookie Francisco Cordero came on in the seventh and promptly loaded the bases with one out, it was starting to look as if clouds would darken the sentiment of the day.

Doug Brocail came in from the bullpen and managed to get the team out of that threat. But there was still a strong sense of unease as the Tigers came to bat in the eighth. The Royals brought in their closer, Jeff Montgomery, to hold the Tigers until Kansas City had its final shot.

A double, a single, and a walk loaded the bases with Fick coming to the plate. He had been up for a brief trial in 1998 and knocked out three homers in just 22 times at bat. He looked like a hitter, too. It's hard to say why, but if you've been around baseball for a while, you just know that someone looks like a hitter by the way he stands at the plate.

The ball Fick hit was still rising when it crashed against the third deck in right field. It was the last grand slam, the last home run of any kind, and the last rally at The Corner. The crowd had seen what it came for and more. The Tigers were ahead 8–2, and after three more outs, the parade of nostalgia could begin.

But now there was one more memory to add for people who thought their Tiger Stadium store was complete. What a way to close a ballpark.

GATES NEVER WAITS (1968)

If the Tigers were trailing, the game had reached the late innings, and the crowd saw Gates Brown begin to stir in the dugout, a low rumble would roll through Tiger Stadium. As he moved to the bat rack, it would begin to gather volume, and when he walked to the on-deck circle, it would swell to a roar. By the time he settled in to hit, the whole place would be in pandemonium.

That's what happened when the man who could step onto the field at any time and turn it all around was primed for action. When the Tigers reached the endgame in 1968, Brown was the one guy everyone wanted to see. His batting average for the year was .370, and as a pinch-hitter it was .462.

If ever cold numbers failed to capture the force a player brought to the game, they would have to be the stats next to Brown's name. Earl Wilson had more home runs and RBIs that year...and he was a pitcher. Only three times in his career did Gates play as many as 100 games in a season. His high-water marks were 15 homers and 54 RBIs. But when it came to the manly art of pinch-hitting, there were few who were better in the game's history.

Gates was one of the most popular players ever to appear for the Tigers. He had come out of a tough background, and an early brush with the law landed him in state prison in Ohio. He learned to joke about it in later years. Once when someone asked him what he had taken in high school, he responded, "Math and overcoats."

Although one of the fastest players on the team, his weak throwing arm relegated him to left field as a starter. But the Tigers had a rising star named Willie Horton who also was scheduled to fill that slot. It wasn't even a matter of the two men, who became close friends, competing for the same slot. Horton was going to be the man, and Brown was going to be the sub. He understood and prepared himself for the even more challenging job of turning into a premier pinch-hitter.

He didn't take to it immediately, although he did serve early notice that he could handle it. In his first time at bat in the major leagues, on June 19, 1963, he pinch hit for Don Mossi and hammered a ball deep into the right-field pavilion at Fenway Park. He was only the third man in American League history to homer in his first time at bat as a pinch-hitter. Since the Tigers were in the midst of a 10-game losing streak, it didn't attract all that much attention. But it was a signifier.

Before 1968, though, Gates hit just .242 as a pinch-hitter. Then he simply exploded. It wasn't so much the number of his hits that year as much as the timing.

In the second game of the season, for example, the Tigers were matched against the defending league champions, the Red Sox, in the opening home series. Boston had edged them by one game in a gut-wrenching finish in 1967, and then the Sox clubbed them again on Opening Day. It looked like the same script all over again.

Denny McLain was making the first start of his historic season in Game 2 and blew a 3–0 lead in the sixth, giving up back-to-back home runs. Jon Warden, making his major league debut, took over in the eighth and managed to hold the Sox, even though the first two hitters he faced reached base.

Now it was the bottom of the ninth with John Wyatt pitching for Boston. The teensy crowd of 6,142, or those few who had remained, barely stirred as Gates moved in to bat for Warden. He drilled the ball into the seats and the Tigers won, 4–3.

No one could have known it at the time, but that game was the harbinger of what was coming. The Tigers went off on a nine-game winning streak and never looked back. The fortunate Warden won twice more, both coming on tenth-inning rallies. He'd been in three big-league games and won all of them.

But the high point of Brown's season may have come in August. By that time Boston had fallen out of the race, and the Tigers were cruising, five and a half games ahead of the Orioles. But the Sox were still dangerous, and Detroit fans knew from experience that no lead ever should be counted on as secure.

The teams had split the first two of the series, and Boston jumped off to a 4–0 lead in the opener of a Sunday doubleheader. The Tigers slowly struggled back, finally tying it in the eighth, while Mayo Smith emptied out his bullpen, trying to control the Sox until the Tigers could pull it out.

Mickey Lolich, sent to the bullpen to fight his way out of his usual midsummer slump, had won the previous night with one and two thirds innings of relief. Now he was called on to throw five more in this game. Lolich was brilliant and his scoreless performance in this game was one of the reasons he was returned to the rotation. But he had reached his limit by the fourteenth.

The Tigers already had received a pinch-homer from an unexpected source. Wayne Comer, a seldom-used outfielder, delivered in the seventh. But Brown was being held in reserve. The Tigers had made just two hits since tying the game, and Boston's Lee Stange retired the first two hitters in the fourteenth without trouble. Then Brown was sent up to hit for Lolich. If the game went any further, Mayo would have to deplete his bullpen even more.

No worries. Brown delivered once more into the seats. The crowd of 49,000 was appreciably larger than the one back in April, and by this time Gates's heroics were expected. They cheered the house down and then, after more than four hours of baseball, settled back expectantly to watch a second game. This time Brown was rewarded with a start in left, batting cleanup.

Exhausted from the opening marathon, the teams were scoreless into the seventh. Then Boston broke through for two. But the Tigers tied it in the eighth, Brown racing home from first with the tying run on a long single by Norm Cash.

"While I was standing on the bag," he said later, "[Boston first baseman] George Scott told me, 'You guys got nothing to worry about. You're gonna win this whole thing easy.'" Brown would help make him a prophet.

The Red Sox went back in front, 5–2, in the ninth, and Warden was summoned to put out the flames. He hadn't won another game since his quick trifecta back in April. But he had turned up in the right spot again.

Four Boston pitchers could not get the Tigers out in the last of the ninth, and four straight hits tied it up. Now here was Brown to face Boston's top left-handed reliever, Sparky Lyle. No homer this time. Instead it was a bouncing single through the right side to win it, 6–5.

Brown had driven in the winning runs in both games on walk-off hits and, incidentally, gave Warden his fourth win. It would be his last in the majors, as arm problems ended his career. But he could honestly say that he owed half his big-league victories to Gates Brown.

Brown never had another year like that one. He only got to bat once in the Series, without a hit. In the seasons since, he has fallen out of the top 10 on the all-time pinch-hit list, too. But for one incredible year, there was never a pinch-hitter like him.

MATCHICK'S MAGIC (1968)

He kind of looked like Huck Finn in spikes: red hair, grin on his face, a boyish enthusiasm whenever he walked onto the field.

Tommy Matchick had no great skills in any one area. But he was a dirty-uniform kind of player. He would do whatever it took to get into a game and win it.

He was part of the three-headed shortstop solution for the Tigers in 1968. He didn't have the range and hands of Ray Oyler. He didn't have the experience and steadiness of Dick Tracewski. As a hitter, he was just marginally better than either one of them. But you had to like the effort.

If it hadn't been for one sultry night at Tiger Stadium, however, his name probably would be part of a trivia game for those trying to recall obscure Detroit shortstops of the past. He'd be one with Coot Veal and Ken Szotkiewicz.

If there was one late rally from that championship season that is remembered best, it is probably Matchick's ninth-inning blast against Baltimore. It was the blow that seemed to summarize the whole unlikely season.

The Orioles had changed managers at the All-Star break and with the new man, Earl Weaver, running the show, they seemed to be reinvigorated. They were still seven and a half games behind the Tigers, and there was a long way to go. Baltimore, which had won it all just two years before, had the talent to catch Detroit. Brooks Robinson and Frank Robinson were still there, as was Boog Powell, and they had added pesky leadoff man Don

Buford. The Orioles traditionally had good pitching, and their staff was anchored by Jim Hardin and Dave McNally; however, their best young pitcher, Jim Palmer, was out with arm problems.

So when they came into Tiger Stadium to start a four-game series on July 19, there was some reason for concern, some eagerness to cut them down before they started getting dangerous ideas.

Weaver decided to go with Wally Bunker, who had thrown a shutout against the Dodgers in the 1966 Series. The Tigers had Mickey Lolich, who was in the middle of his usual midsummer sag. Frank Robinson crashed a two-run homer off him in the third, and the Orioles tacked on two more in the sixth.

More than 53,000 fans were in the stadium for this Friday night game and they had heard this song before. Failure had been a far more familiar figure in Detroit than success in recent years. The Tigers themselves acknowledged that they had blown the pennant the previous year. Now they could see it slipping away once more.

The Tigers didn't even have a hit when they came to bat in the sixth. They looked listless, overmatched. But after a walk, Dick McAuliffe connected with a two-run shot into the stands. One hit had halved the lead. This might get interesting yet.

Going into the ninth, however, nothing had changed. The Detroit bullpen held the Orioles, but after their scoring spurt, the Tigers had gone back into hitless mode against reliever Eddie Watt. It was still 4–2. Gates Brown, their best pinch-hitter, already had come into the game and struck out. If they were going to pull this one out, it would take a touch of magic.

But when Jim Northrup started the inning with a single and Al Kaline walked, the big crowd suddenly became involved again. Lefty John O'Donoghue was called in to deal with the dangerous Norm Cash and got him on a force at second. Now it was time for the closer, Moe Drabowsky.

After a lackluster career as a starter, Drabowsky had been turned into a short relief man when he came to Baltimore in 1966 from the Kansas City A's. He was a great practical joker whose favorite prop was a rubber snake. He also knew the bullpen phone number in Kansas City, and after being traded, he put in a call and

Tommy Matchick had no great skills in any one area, but a home run he hit against the Orioles in 1968 symbolized the Tigers' memorable season. Photo courtesy of Getty Images.

told the coach to get one of the A's relievers up and throwing. This came as quite a surprise to their manager in the distant dugout. When Drabowsky was revealed as the culprit, the KC coaching staff was not amused.

But it was his arm rather than his wit that brought him to Baltimore. He was signed on the recommendation of Brooks Robinson, who said he could not get around on Drabowsky's hard stuff. When Drabowsky struck out six Dodgers in a row in the first game of the '66 Series, the wisdom of that choice seemed confirmed.

Now he was in to snuff out the Tigers. He got Bill Freehan on a force. Northrup scored, making it 4–3, but all the Tigers had left to send up was Matchick. It looked like a huge mismatch. As the best hitter among the Detroit shortstops, he was barely over .200. He did bat left-handed, but that didn't seem to cut much ice against Drabowsky.

The ball Matchick hit started out looking like a moderately deep fly to right. Frank Robinson was backing up and seemed to have a bead on it.

The official distance down the right-field line at Tiger Stadium was 325 feet. That's what the white numbers said on the wall, at least. But that didn't account for the overhang, the first row of upper-deck boxes that extended out over the field. That shortened the distance by a few feet.

Whatever the difference in actual length was, it was just enough. Matchick's fly ball scraped the overhang as Robinson stood helplessly below. Matchick circled the bases behind Freehan, and the Tigers halted the charging Orioles 5–4.

But not really. The Birds left town on Sunday just five and a half games behind, after taking the next three from Detroit. If Matchick hadn't connected, though, the lead would have been down to three and a half, and who knows what would have happened then?

It gave the Tigers the breathing room they needed. When they went into Baltimore the following weekend and took two out of three, the lead was back up to six and a half. A week's worth of work had shaved just half a game off the Detroit lead.

Matchick would hit just two more home runs in his entire major league career, which ended four seasons later. It is fairly safe to say that neither compared to this one.

SPRINGTIME BLOSSOMS

The stars who emerge during spring training don't always stick when the games begin to count. Their careers can flame out in a hurry. One case in point was John Baumgartner, a sensation in Florida in 1953. He was installed as the regular third baseman on Opening Day, made two errors, and after seven games was hitting .185. He was sent to the minors and was never heard from again.

Another early sensation was Purnal Goldy, who was the terror of the exhibition season in 1962 and touted as the next Al Kaline. He lasted 29 games before disappearing for good.

BERGMAN'S BLAST (1984)

Everyone remembers the 35–5 beginning, the impetus that powered the wire-to-wire run of the 1984 Tigers. What is not so well recalled is that when that streak was done and the season moved into June, the Tigers were still not in command of the race. Snapping right at their heels was a young, aggressive Toronto team.

It took Dave Bergman's tenth-inning home run in a classic showdown to finally put the pursuers in their place.

The Blue Jays were in their ninth season since joining the league as an expansion team and had put together their first contender. They would threaten almost every year thereafter before breaking through with consecutive championships in 1992 and 1993. But in 1984 they were knocking on the door for the first time.

That was making Sparky Anderson very nervous. "If we had blown the pennant after the start we had, they'd have come and hanged me," the manager said later, adding, "and I would have deserved it."

After the burst from the gate tapered off, the Tigers won just three of their next nine. So the first time the teams met, on a Monday night in Detroit, the Jays trailed by only four and a half games. Ordinarily that would be a nice margin so early in the season. But it was not what you'd expect after the start the Tigers had. The Jays also had won 19 straight one-run games and were playing with loads of confidence.

Enthusiasm had built early in Detroit, and this season would establish a Tiger Stadium attendance record of 2.7 million. In the memories of most fans, this game was played before a packed ballpark. Actually it was only half filled, with about 26,000 customers. Mondays are Mondays, a down day even in great seasons.

Anderson chose one of his secondary starters, Juan Berenguer, to pitch this one. He threw hard and could be overpowering when the moon was right. He could also be all over the lot, and Sparky never knew which version he was going to get. Under the guidance of pitching coach Roger Craig, Berenguer had become somewhat more consistent. But he was still just a 3–3 pitcher and he was going up against Toronto's ace, Dave Stieb.

Anderson had stacked his lineup because Stieb's slider was especially tough on right-handed hitters. He never hesitated to come inside, and he regularly led the league in hit batters. So every lefty on the bench got a start, including Howard Johnson at third base and Bergman at first. Both were part of triple-platoon arrangements at those positions. Bergman also would come in frequently as a defensive replacement. Sparky had just the opposite problem with Johnson, who would often leave games in favor of Tom Brookens's glove.

Bergman was with his fourth big-league team, the quintessential journeyman—never quite hitting well enough to play regularly, but a good man to have around. He'd been with the Giants the previous year and was dealt to Philadelphia in the off-season. Before ever playing a game with the Phillies, though, he was traded to Detroit during spring training along with a left-handed reliever, Willie Hernandez. The deal turned out to be the final piece of the puzzle for the Tigers, as Hernandez walked away with the Cy Young Award. But this was to be Bergman's night.

"Darrell Evans had been with the Giants with me and he came to Detroit as a big free-agent signing," said Bergman. "When I walked in the clubhouse door in Florida after being traded, he called me aside and said, 'Something special is going on here.'" That turned out to be an understatement.

In this game, however, Anderson's strategy was not fazing Stieb. He gassed the Tigers through six while the Jays were building a 3–0 lead behind homers from Willie Upshaw and George Bell. Aside from the long balls, it had been a good effort for Berenguer, too.

But in the seventh the Tigers struck with sudden alacrity. Chet Lemon was hit by a pitch, Bergman singled, and Johnson, who would go on to star with the Mets for several years, put one off the right-field foul pole. In a twinkling, the Tigers had tied it, 3–3.

Now it became a chess game, as the bullpens took over and each manager switched relievers, batter by batter. Hernandez wiggled out of a man on third with a no-out situation in the eighth, getting a pop-up, an infield grounder, and a strikeout. Left-hander Jimmy Key did the same for the Jays in the ninth, getting a critical out with two runners aboard.

Toronto went down in order in the tenth, with right-hander Aurelio Lopez picking up for Hernandez to get the final out. When Detroit put a runner on second with one out, Jays manager Bobby Cox pulled the same kind of switch. He brought in his own right-hander, Roy Lee Jackson, to pick up for Key. Sparky had used his entire left-handed bench as starters and had no one left to come in against Jackson.

Roy Lee got Rusty Kuntz on a comeback grounder. But then he made a critical mistake. He walked Lemon—and that brought up Bergman, with two on and two out.

"I'd played winter ball with Roy Lee and knew what he threw," said Bergman. "But it was more than that. There comes a time in every season when a hitter gets his mechanics together, and this was that night for me."

Bergman had been on base when Johnson connected and also had walked. Now he and Jackson engaged in what many observers called the greatest time at bat they ever had witnessed. The count went to 3–2, with Jackson just missing the outside corner on the pitch that sent it full

Jackson then threw everything he had in his arsenal for strikes, and Bergman kept fouling them off. Seven pitches in a row. Bergman said later he was so locked in that the only thing he was afraid of was that Jackson would walk him.

On the 13th pitch Jackson's luck ran out. Bergman's hit went on a line into the right-field upper deck. The Tigers won 6–3 on Bergman's first home run of the season.

It has always been remembered as the blow that deflated the Jays. But memory can be deceptive. They turned around and won the next two games in Detroit. It was only when Ruppert Jones, called up from the minors just two days before, cracked yet another three-run homer for the Tigers on Thursday afternoon to win that one that the Jays realized they were chasing phantoms. Toronto started to slide back in the standings and was never a factor in the race after that.

But the drama surrounding Bergman's blast made it the more lasting image. It's hard to argue why it shouldn't be.

NO HITS AND A WIN (1967)

No one has yet figured out how to get shut out and still win a ballgame. But on a Sunday afternoon in Baltimore in 1967, the Tigers did the next best thing. They became only the second team in major league history to have a no-hitter thrown at them and win. It was a game that truly wasn't over 'til it was over.

It had happened a few times when a no-hit game went into extra innings. Pittsburgh's Harvey Haddix even lost a 12-inning perfect game against Milwaukee in 1959. But until the Tigers turned the trick, only one team ever had done it in nine. Cincinnati pulled it off, 1–0, in a 1964 game against Houston's Ken Johnson.

The Tigers made it even tougher on themselves, though. They actually were trailing 1–0 when they put together an improbable last-ditch rally in the ninth without ever getting a hit.

The game had an even greater resonance at the time because Baltimore was the defending world champion. The Orioles had handled Detroit easily the previous season, but many experts were picking the Tigers as the team most likely to overturn Baltimore in 1967. So the first trip into the Charm City in late April was fraught with significance, even this early in the season.

The teams split the first two games of the series, and in the opener of a Sunday doubleheader it would be Earl Wilson for the Tigers against Steve Barber.

Barber had come to the majors with a hard fastball, described by his catchers as feeling like a brick when it hit their mitts. Future Hall of Famer Jim Palmer remembered watching Barber pitch and wondering how he'd ever be able to reach the majors "if you had to throw that hard to make it."

Barber was the first 20-game winner in Orioles franchise history, but he was always struggling with control problems along the way. He'd developed tendonitis in his pitching elbow in 1966, which kept him out of the Series. But when the new season began, he was still regarded as an integral part of the best pitching staff in the league.

He was now in his eighth season but still threw hard enough to discourage hitters from digging in. This game turned out to be wilder than most for Barber.

He walked 10 batters, hit two, threw two wild pitches, and was constantly in trouble. Runners were on base in every inning except one, and one such uprising was aided by Barber's own error. But no one could get a hit off him, and the Tigers couldn't score.

Meanwhile, Wilson was adding to the drama by pitching a gem of a game himself. Going into the eighth, he was working on a two-hit shutout. But then strange things began happening. He walked the bases full, including a pass to Barber after the Tigers had walked a pinch-hitter intentionally to get at him. Manager Hank Bauer refused to pull Barber for another pinch-hitter; not while he was working on a no-hit game, even one as bizarre as this.

Leadoff man Luis Aparicio then delivered a sacrifice fly, and the Orioles had a 1–0 lead without getting a hit to accomplish it. But the Tigers were paying attention and taking notes.

Norm Cash and Ray Oyler, the weakest hitter among the Tigers, drew Barber's eighth and ninth walks of the game to open the ninth. Wilson, one of the best-hitting pitchers in the game, was also allowed to bat for himself, and he put down a perfect sacrifice bunt. Now the tying run was on third. But when dangerous Willie Horton popped up, it appeared as if Barber was going to get out of it. There was only Mickey Stanley left to get.

Pinch runner Dick Tracewski edged off the bag at third as Barber went into his delivery. And he threw a wild pitch. The ball bounced away from catcher Larry Haney, who had just entered the game, and Tracewski scampered home to tie it, 1–1. It was such a shocking turn of events that every writer in the press box leaped to their feet in astonishment.

When Barber walked Stanley too, Bauer had seen enough. He brought in relief specialist Stu Miller to close things out and take the game into the home half of the ninth. Bauer had made another change this inning as well. He'd brought rookie shortstop Mark Belanger, regarded as an outstanding defensive player, into the game. But he put him in at second base.

Miller did his job, getting Don Wert to hit a bouncer to Aparicio at short. He flipped to second for the force—and Belanger dropped the ball. Stanley slid in safely, and Detroit's second run scored from third. The Tigers still hadn't made a hit, but now they were ahead 2–1. When Al Kaline ended the inning with a force-out, the scenario was complete.

Reliever Fred Gladding didn't spoil it, retiring the Orioles in order. The Tigers had won, and manager Mayo Smith spent the time between games preparing his scorecard to send off to Cooperstown.

The Tigers won the second game, too, as the discombobulated Orioles couldn't pull themselves together. As it turned out, injuries mounted for Baltimore, and they were not a factor in the hectic 1967 pennant race. Barber was never able to regain his previous form and went to the Yankees in a midseason deal. He spent most of his remaining career working out of the bullpen for five other teams.

But he never again pitched in a game quite as weird as this one.

MAGIC MOMENT (1968)

The Tigers won an incredible 27 games on last at-bats in 1968. It was one year when it never seemed to be over 'til it was over, even when it came to clinching the pennant. In many regards, that might have been the biggest of all the last-ditch hits.

The Yankees were in town for the big night. It was Tuesday, September 17, and 46,000 fans were on hand to watch the Tigers end 23 years of frustration and win their first pennant since 1945, their first in the age of television.

It was only fitting that the Yankees should be the foils, too. They had ruined so many summers for Detroit fans with their incessant excellence. In those 23 seasons New York had won 15 times. But now they were reduced to the role of also-rans.

Joe Sparma started for the Tigers. He had been a disappointment in this otherwise wonderful year. A 16-game winner the previous season, the former Ohio State quarterback seemed to have finally conquered the control problems that had held him back. But he lapsed back into old habits and went off on manager Mayo Smith in the media for taking him out early in a game at Cleveland the previous month. At 8–10, he was now a question mark.

"I can't start him and because of his control I can't pitch him in relief," grumbled Mayo. "What am I supposed to do? Shoot him?"

But on this night, Sparma was everything he was supposed to be. He was not overthrowing the ball and had the Yankees hitting harmless grounders all night.

Detroit's magic number was one. If they won this game, or if Baltimore lost to Boston, the race would be over. Adding to the interest was a promotion that the *Detroit Free Press* was running. Pick the exact moment, the hour and minute, that the pennant was clinched and you won two tickets to all the Series games. The paper had received tens of thousands of entries, and the contest was the night's backstory.

Denny McLain, his head covered in shaving cream, pours a bottle of champagne over the head of teammate Al Kaline as they celebrate their American League pennant in the dressing room on September 17, 1968.

UNHITTABLE HERNANDEZ

The clearest evidence that the magic of 1984 was gone the next year was the performance of Willie Hernandez. When he entered a game during the championship season, it meant the story was over. He saved 32 of them, won nine more, and opponents hit just .194 against him.

On the surface 1985 wasn't such a big drop-off. He saved 31 and won eight. But he also lost 10 times within a three-month span in midseason, which is the deadliest stat any closer can accumulate. The clincher came when he was called in to protect a 6–2 lead in California in late August and ended up surrendering five runs and taking the loss.

The Tigers finished 15 games out of first and weren't in the race for most of the summer. Hernandez became the focus of fan frustration. By the end of the year, the defending Cy Young Award winner was jeered every time he entered a game and was never an effective closer again. That's when everyone knew that 1984 was really over.

Going into the ninth, Sparma knocked in the only run of the evening himself. He picked up his roommate and friend Bill Freehan with a single in the fifth. He had held the Yankees hitless between the first and eighth innings, and the fans were already stirring in anticipation of party time.

In this era before text messaging and other electronic gizmos, no one in the stands knew what was going on in the Baltimore game. All they were told on the radio was that Boston was holding a 2–0 lead in the late innings. In fact, as the Yankees came to bat in the ninth, the Orioles had already lost. The magic moment had struck. But there was no message on the scoreboard, and Ernie Harwell was asked to say nothing on the radio.

Then the Yankees almost went and spoiled everything. With the Tigers just an out away from the win, Jake Gibbs rammed a single up the middle off Sparma to drive in the tying run. He finished the inning, but the Tigers were coming to bat as the American League champions. Management feared, however, if they didn't win it now, the word would get out and the celebratory joy might become unconfined...and dangerous.

Reliever Steve Hamilton got two quick outs, and the Tigers resigned themselves to having to post the Baltimore score. Then Al Kaline drew a pinch-hit walk, and when Freehan singled, he raced around to third. Kaline hadn't been playing regularly, but when he left the house that afternoon he told his wife, Louise, "I have a feeling I'm going to do something special tonight."

Now it was Gates Brown pinch hitting, and the crowd screamed for a hit. But new pitcher Lindy McDaniel walked him to load the bases and bring Don Wert to the plate. It had been a rough year for the third baseman. After several good seasons, he was barely hitting .200, and the big crowd's expectations sank.

Wert reached for an outside pitch, though, and looped a single that barely cleared the second baseman's head. Kaline, fulfilling his earlier prediction, raced home with the run that...well, if it didn't really win the pennant, it still gave the Tigers and their fans a moment that was just as great as if it had.

WHEELIN' AND DEALIN'

TWO GUYS NAMED DEMETER (1960, 1966)

You remember the bad trades most vividly. That's just human nature. But the Tigers have made some pretty good deals throughout the years, and a few of them even resulted in pennants. Two of the best led directly to the 1968 championship. By an odd quirk, both involved Detroit giving up a player named Demeter.

The first one ranks among the franchise's all-time steals. The Tigers picked up Norm Cash, a future batting champ and one of the top sluggers ever to play in Detroit. The price was a minor league third baseman, Steve Demeter.

Frank Lane was the Cleveland general manager and was famous for his willingness to trade anyone, anywhere, anytime. He had picked up Cash from the White Sox as a throw-in on a deal that returned the great outfielder Minnie Minoso to Chicago.

Cash had not caused much of a stir as a utility man on the 1959 White Sox pennant-winning team. Lane really had no plans for him in Cleveland either. He was, however, concerned about infield defense, so he was willing to look at Demeter.

The trade was made during spring training of 1960 and attracted little attention. The real blockbuster came a few days later when Lane dared to trade matinee idol Rocky Colavito to the Tigers in return for defending batting champ Harvey Kuenn. The deal was the most controversial in the history of both teams. It was debated for years and credited with destroying fan support for the Indians.

The Tigers traded a minor league third baseman for Norm Cash, who became a batting champ and one of the top sluggers ever to play in Detroit.
Photo courtesy of Getty Images.

It turned out, however, the real headliner was the unnoticed Cash. In his second season in Detroit, he won the batting title with a .361 average and teamed with Colavito to hit 86 homers. The Tigers chased the Yankees all season before falling back in September, and the team was set at first base for the next decade and a half. Demeter? He played four games for Cleveland and never got a hit.

The second trade was pulled off midway through the 1966 season. The Tigers had two brilliant young pitchers in Mickey Lolich and Denny McLain. But no one had stepped up to take the third spot in the rotation. They also had some young outfielders who needed to play regularly. That made center fielder Don Demeter excess baggage.

Demeter had come over two years earlier in an especially bad trade that sent Hall of Famer Jim Bunning to the Phillies.

"Charlie Dressen [Detroit's manager] loved National Leaguers, especially ex-Dodgers," said pitcher Hank Aguirre in analyzing the deal a few years later. "He thought they played the game right. So we kept making deals for them—Demeter, Larry Sherry, Johnny Podres, Dick Tracewski. We got burned a few times, too."

Demeter was regarded as a serviceable outfielder, although overly cautious. But he never posted the slugging stats the Tigers had anticipated. Detroit was eyeing Earl Wilson, a decent pitcher on a dreadful Boston staff, and the Red Sox needed a center fielder to play between their young stars, Carl Yastrzemski and Tony Conigliaro.

Wilson was 31 and not developing into the stopper Boston needed. So the deal was made. Wilson promptly won 35 games in the next season and a half, and his big home-run swing turned him into a fan favorite. He thrived in Detroit and went on to win 13 for the 1968 pennant winners, starting Game 3 of the World Series. Demeter lasted one year in Boston, was traded, and retired at the end of 1967.

By the way, no other players named Demeter have ever played in the major leagues.

HEINIE AND THE ALEXANDERS (1927, 1932, 1987)

It was acknowledged earlier that the very worst trade the Tigers ever made was the giveaway of Billy Pierce. But there are some competitors for that distinction. One involves a current Hall of Famer, and the other a probable future Hall of Famer—both of them leaving town with only slight benefits in return.

The Tigers were accustomed to having a full supply of hard-hitting outfielders in the 1920s. In fact, the 1926 aggregation was so good that they forced manager Ty Cobb to put himself on the bench. This trio consisted of Harry Heilmann, Bob "Fats" Fothergill, and Heinie Manush. The first two hit .367 that year and all Manush did was lead the league at .378. Cobb? He could only manage a paltry .339 in what was to be his final season with the Tigers.

Heilmann had already won three batting titles and would add one more before he was through. But it was the 25-year-old Manush who seemed to have the most promise. He was already in his fourth year with Detroit and had improved each season. He was in line to take over permanently from the great Cobb at the heart of the Tigers' lineup.

Manush was, in fact, a special project of Cobb's. "He made Heinie a great hitter," recalled Charlie Gehringer. "He had a habit of holding his hands too high so that he'd uppercut the ball. Every time he'd start doing it again, Cobb would whistle at him from the dugout as a reminder. Of course, he also had the talent to take advantage of it."

Manush also appealed to Cobb because he was a throwback hitter, a slap and slasher who choked up on the bat in the era when the long ball had come into vogue. Cobb detested the long ball and adopted Manush as one of his own. It also didn't hurt that he was a fellow Southerner from Alabama.

In 1927 Cobb departed for Philadelphia and Manush went into a funk. His average dropped 80 points to .298, and while his other stats were good, management figured that maybe he wouldn't be the same hitter without his mentor around.

So at the end of the season he was dealt to the Browns in return for outfielder Harry Rice, pitcher Elam Vangilder, and shortstop Chick Galloway. None of them ever amounted to much in Detroit.

And Manush? He went right back up to .378 again the next year and lost a second batting title by a fraction of a point on the very last day of the season to Goose Goslin. He finished his career with a .330 lifetime average and went into Cooperstown in 1964.

A few years later, the Tigers dealt away yet another batting champion. Only this time it was a champion to be. Dale Alexander was nicknamed Moose, which should give you some idea of his size and agility, or lack thereof, at first base. He had one of the greatest rookie years of all time in 1929, hitting .343, driving in 137 runs, and belting a team-record 25 home runs.

His figures were almost as good the next year, but in 1931, while still hitting .325, his power stroke vanished. He hit just three homers.

The Tigers realized belatedly that the long ball was not just a passing fad, as Cobb had insisted. Winning teams had lots of smash in their lineups, and Alexander's power decline was not what Detroit was counting on. So when he started 1932 hitting .250, he was gone, traded to Boston for outfielder Earl Webb.

MORE TERRIBLE TRADES

- 1963: Jim Bunning was sent to the Phillies for Don Demeter. Bunning went on to solidify his Hall of Fame credentials with 74 wins in the next four years.
- 1999: Juan Gonzalez came from Texas for a package of six players. He stayed one year and spent most of it complaining about the dimensions of Comerica Park.
- 1959: Larry Doby arrived from the White Sox for Tito Francona. Doby was almost finished, while Francona hit .363 that season and led the league in doubles the following year.
- At various times the Tigers also had Carl Hubbell, Rip Sewell, and Maury Wills in their minor league system. They passed on all three.

It wasn't all that terrible a deal. Webb was a power hitter who had just set the big-league record for doubles—a record that still stands—with 67. He even seemed to be an upgrade over the weakened Moose. Besides, the Tigers had a young first baseman coming up fast through the minors, and management thought he was just one year away from Detroit. His name was Hank Greenberg.

Wouldn't you know it? Alexander found things highly agreeable in Boston and went on a hitting tear. Although the power numbers never came back, he finished the year at .367, which was good for the batting title. Webb never panned out in Detroit and one year later was out of the majors.

But so was Alexander. A previous leg injury was aggravated by burns he suffered in a diathermy machine, and when gangrene set in, his career in the majors was finished. Even though the Tigers had coughed up a batting champ, the deal was kind of a push.

Fifty-five years later, though, another deal involving a player named Alexander was a bit more controversial. Well, a lot more, really.

The Tigers were involved in a tight race in 1987, contesting the divisional title with Toronto. As the summer wore on, it became apparent that they were in need of pitching help. General manager Jim Campbell's philosophy was if you have a chance to win a pennant, go for it, because there was no guarantee the chance would come again.

There was also a strong precedent for making the deal. In 1972, in a similarly close race, the Tigers had turned to the National League and plucked off left-hander Woodie Fryman on waivers. He went 10–3 down the stretch and made the difference in the race, although Oakland took out the Tigers in the playoffs.

A similar scenario was developing in 1987, and the Tigers began eyeing the situation in Atlanta. The Braves were not very good, and one of their veteran starters, Doyle Alexander, was disgruntled. Being disgruntled was pretty much a constant for Alexander, who was noted for his sullen disposition. He had been kicking around for 15 years, though, had won 17 games on three occasions, and had gone through pennant races before.

Alexander came to Detroit and was brilliant, going 9–0 and carrying Detroit into the playoffs. Once again they were eliminated before getting to the main show, however, and that season was the start of a 19-year absence from postseason play.

Moreover, the price turned out to be steep. The Braves demanded one of the farm system's jewels, pitcher John Smoltz. He reached the majors the following year and became a mainstay of a staff that carried the Braves into every playoff between 1991 and 2005—except for the strike year of 1994.

The trade had succeeded in its original intent. But sometimes the cost of immediate success may be long-term disaster. Twenty years after the trade was made and Alexander was long gone, Smoltz was still going strong in Atlanta and had been to five World Series.

Bad trade. Case closed.

ROGERS THROWS BLANKS (2006)

When the Tigers decided to make Kenny Rogers their big free-agent pickup for 2006, the almost universal reaction in Detroit was "Huh?"

What was that about? Sure, Rogers had some decent years in the past. But he was 41 years old on a team that was supposed to be assembling a young pitching staff. He had been involved in a scuffle with a TV cameraman in Texas the previous season, and when he appeared at the All-Star Game in Detroit shortly afterward, he was roundly booed.

Who needed this?

But under the greatest possible pressure, it was Rogers who came through for the Tigers. His two scoreless starts in the postseason put them into the World Series and gave them a modicum of respect once they were there.

Much more than that, however, it was a matter of personal vindication. Rogers had been down this route once before. Exactly ten years prior, in 1996, he was the big free-agent catch of the Yankees. He had run off several good seasons with Texas, and the thinking in New York was that sharp left-handers usually prospered at Yankee Stadium.

Kenny Rogers's three straight shutouts in the 2006 postseason put the Tigers into the World Series. Photo courtesy of Getty Images.

It didn't happen. He was only so-so for the Yankees during their pennant drive that year, and in his three postseason starts he was a mess. In just seven innings of work he gave up 11 runs. He was almost as bad three years later when he pitched for the Mets. In the 1999 playoffs he pitched 12 innings and gave up nine runs.

His two Big Apple experiences were not something Rogers liked to dwell on. Among the New York media, which do so much to shape national opinion, he was dismissed as a pitcher who folds in the clutch.

Now it was a chilly October night with a big full moon hanging over Comerica Park for the biggest game in the brief history of the stadium. The teams had split the first two games in New York. Whoever won this time would take a stranglehold on the best-of-five series.

The capacity crowd was riding an emotional high. The Tigers had overcome a 3–1 New York lead in Game 2 against Mike Mussina, a pitcher who usually toyed with them. Now it was another old nemesis, Randy Johnson, on the mound to oppose Rogers in a battle of the over-40 pitchers.

But it was quickly obvious that back problems had turned the once-formidable Johnson into a fairly ordinary pitcher. Detroit

FOUR GREAT DEALS

- 2005: Placido Polanco was obtained from the Phillies for Ugueth Urbina, who was then convicted of attempted homicide in Venezuela and sentenced to 14 years in prison.
- 1984: Willie Hernandez came over from the Phillies for outfielder Glenn Wilson and immediately won the Cy Young Award.
- 2004: Carlos Guillen joined the team for utility infielder Ramon Santiago and turned into a force at shortstop.
- 1970: Eddie Brinkman, Aurelio Rodriguez, and Joe Coleman Jr. were pried loose from Washington for Denny McLain, forming the core of the division champions two years later.

reached him for three runs in the second inning, all on well-hit singles, and the ballpark was rocking.

Detroit had faltered badly down the stretch. After leading the Central Division by a comfortable margin for almost the entire season, they lost their final five in a row. In the season-ending series with a dreadful Kansas City team, they were swept, allowing Minnesota to brush past them into first place. The Tigers had to settle for the wild-card slot, and the opponent now would be the dreaded Yankees—with the best record in the league.

Rogers had lost two games in the final week, hit hard both times. In fact, he was just 6–5 after the All-Star Game to finish the year at 17–8. He had a history of second-half slumps, and some media commentators were urging manager Jim Leyland to get him out of the rotation.

But here he was in the pivotal game of the divisional playoffs, pitching like a man possessed. Every time the Yankees even suggested a threat, he stomped it out like Smokey the Bear at a campfire. He was working the corners of the plate, striking out eight Yankees. Most of them came with men on base.

More than that, though, was Rogers's demeanor. He was practically screaming for the ball when he thought Pudge Rodriguez was too slow in getting it back to him. He could hardly wait to throw the next pitch. The fans picked up on his emotion, and from the middle of the game on, the ballpark was seething with hysteria. After every strikeout, strangers were high-fiving each other, shouting at the top of their lungs as if the big moon above had truly turned them into lunatics.

It was not only Rogers getting a little back. It was everyone who had followed the Tigers through all the recent seasons of frustration, watching the Yankees get to one World Series after another while the lights of the Detroit ballpark stayed dark.

By the eighth inning, no one was seated. By now the lead had grown to 6–0, and it was as if everyone was trying to will Rogers home. He struck out Johnny Damon and Bobby Abreu around a walk. But with the always dangerous Alex Rodriguez coming to bat, Leyland waved in the flame-throwing setup man, Joel Zumaya. Rogers walked off to the greatest ovation Comerica ever had heard.

It was as if yesterday's ghosts had finally been exorcised for him. No one would dare question his heart after this performance.

But Rogers wasn't finished. After the Tigers disposed of the Yankees the next day, he started Game 3 against Oakland. Detroit was already up in this Series, two games to none. But he was, if anything, even more tightly focused. This time he gave the A's only two hits into the eighth, and the Tigers put them away, 3–0.

Then it was time for the main event, and Rogers's supply of blanks was far from exhausted. He had thrown 15 frames of them in the playoffs and had plenty left for St. Louis. He also had something else. Cards manager Tony LaRussa popped out of the dugout in the first inning of Game 2 and called for the umpires to look at something on Rogers's throwing hand.

It was a 40-degree night in Detroit, and Rogers said it was nothing more nefarious than dirt to keep his hand warm. The umpires didn't press the point and permitted him to wash it off and stay in the game. No one had seen anything suspicious in the previous two shutouts. But LaRussa, who had gone to law school and was a master gamesman, had made his point.

If he intended to rattle Rogers, though, the attempt was a miserable failure. He stopped the Cards on another two-hitter over eight full innings, extending his postseason shutout streak to 23. St. Louis finally reached closer Todd Jones for a run in the ninth, but it was Detroit's only win in the error-plagued Series.

So the pitcher who started the season in Detroit with an indifferent "huh" ended it with a big "hurrah."

GRABBING A GREAT 1946 [1946]

There are eight players in baseball's Hall of Fame who spent most of their careers with the Tigers. Out of that group, only one arrived through a trade. So the acquisition of George Kell in 1946 has to go down as one of the best deals the franchise ever made.

The Tigers not only got one of the top hitters in the league but the best defensive third baseman of his era. In addition, he remained closely identified with the team for years as a television play-by-play man. His pairing with Al Kaline is still regarded as the best and most knowledgeable combination on the tube.

All that was gravy, though. All the Tigers really wanted was someone who could simply plug a hole at third base. Pinky Higgins had been the starter at that position for six years, but when he came back from the war in 1946, it became apparent that at 37 years old he was not the same player.

The trade for George Kell in 1946 is considered one of the best moves the Tigers ever made. Photo courtesy of Getty Images.

The Tigers also had come to that conclusion about Barney McCosky. He had been a deadly hitter in his first four years with the Tigers, one of the key players on the 1940 pennant-winning team. But he, too, had been a soldier, and when he got back, it was clear that something was lost.

Detroit had won a pennant in 1945 with Bob Maier and Jimmy Outlaw playing third. But that was wartime, and neither one seemed capable of filling the position with the tougher competition coming in.

Kell played for the Philadelphia A's for two years during the war and seemed to improve steadily. But he looked like a .270 hitter, and Connie Mack had dealt for the more powerful Hank Majeski to play third. The chance to pick up McCosky was too good to pass up. So they made the swap—Kell for McCosky even up.

Kell won a batting title in 1949, twice led the league in hits, drove in 101 runs in 1950 despite hitting just eight home runs, and played the position brilliantly. Meanwhile, chronic back problems ended McCosky's career as a regular within two years.

Kell was the central figure in one of the most dramatic batting races in history. In 1949 Ted Williams seemed to have the third triple crown of his career, an unprecedented feat, all but wrapped

SKIPPER SWICHEROO

The most bizarre swap in Detroit's history didn't involve players. Tigers CEO Bill DeWitt and Cleveland's general manager Frank Lane decided they had already exhausted those options in 1960. They had dealt Norm Cash, Rocky Colavito, and Harvey Kuenn to each other in April.

By August, however, it was clear that neither team was going anywhere. Cleveland was in fourth place, and the Tigers were sixth. So they simply decided to trade managers. Jimmy Dykes went to the Indians, and Joe Gordon came to Detroit.

It turned out to be a pretty even deal. Dykes went 26–32 in Cleveland, and Gordon was 26–31 in Detroit and was fired at the end of the year.

up. In late September he had a 10-point lead over Kell, who had been sidelined with injuries for much of the month.

But the summer of '49 was also one of the classic pennant races of all time, with the Yankees closing fast to nip Boston on the final weekend. So Williams was playing under the greatest pressure imaginable and drawing walks almost every other time at bat.

Kell kept drawing closer, but on the last day he still trailed Williams by two points. The Yankees and the Red Sox were in a dead heat and whichever team won on that day won the pennant. The Tigers were out of the race but they had to face one of the league's top pitchers, Cleveland's Bob Lemon.

But Kell singled and doubled against him. Bob Feller came into the game to pitch relief and struck out Kell. It was just the 13th time he had struck out all year, the fewest ever for a batting champion. Then he flied out to left.

Word came into the press box in the ninth inning that Williams had gone zero-for-two with two walks in Boston's loss. The Detroit writers did some quick calculations and figured out that if Kell batted again and made an out, Williams would win the title. If Kell didn't bat in the ninth, however, he would win by almost two ten-thousandths of a percentage point. It was .34390 for Kell and .34375 for Williams.

They called that information to the dugout. When he heard it, manager Red Rolfe, who called Kell "my seven-day-a-week player," made up his mind that if Kell was scheduled to bat, he would pinch hit for him.

But when Kell heard about it, he refused. "You didn't beat out Ted Williams at anything too often, and if this was going to be my chance, I wanted to do it the right way," he said later.

With one out, Dick Wakefield singled for the Tigers. That brought up Eddie Lake, with Kell in the on-deck circle. Trying to focus his mind, he watched Lake settle in and hit a ground ball straight at Cleveland shortstop Ray Boone. Boone stepped on second, fired to first for the double play, and the season was over. Kell threw his bat in the air and let out a whoop of relief. He hadn't backed in and had won it the right way.

Kell would go on to play for the Red Sox, the White Sox, and the Orioles—getting voted to start the All-Star Game on every one of those teams. He had led all vote-getters in 1950 with the Tigers. The Orioles acquired him for the main purpose of tutoring their promising young third baseman, Brooks Robinson. Kell seems to have done a good job with that.

He retired after the 1957 season, an old 35 with bad legs, but still steady enough to hit .297. Then he waited. He was assured that election to Cooperstown would come, but somehow it never happened. At that time, the only Hall of Fame third baseman who had spent most of his career in the American League was Home Run Baker.

"Never playing in a World Series hurt and so did the fact that I was traded so often in my last few seasons," he said. "But I never gave up hope."

After 26 years the word finally came through from the Old-Timers Committee in 1983. With poetic justice, he entered the Hall in the same class as his prize pupil, Robinson.

A TOUCH OF VIOLENCE

AND THE BAND PLAYED ON (1967)

There may not have been a worse day in the history of Detroit, or the Tigers, than July 23, 1967. On an afternoon when the city was going up in flames, scene of the worst urban riots of the decade, the Tigers were playing a Sunday doubleheader with the Yankees, as if everything was normal.

Historians tell us that the emperor Nero played the fiddle while Rome burned. In Detroit the music was supplied by the organ in Tiger Stadium.

The team was involved in one of the tightest pennant races in baseball history, a race that wouldn't be decided until the last pitch of the last game of the season. At this point, there were five teams within two games of each other, with Detroit tied for fourth behind the front-running White Sox.

Nearly 35,000 fans had come to watch the crucial doubleheader with the last-place Yankees. None of them knew what was going on just a few miles from the ballpark up 12th Street.

Early that morning police had raided an illegal after-hours establishment, a "blind pig." It was a sultry night, and people were out on the street for a breath of fresh air. A crowd gathered around the cops, and the mood quickly grew tense. Someone threw a bottle, and the riot was on.

Police and city officials decided the best course was to put a lid on information in the hopes of restricting the violence to a few blocks. So when fans made their way to the ballpark early that afternoon, no one had any idea what was going on.

Early in the first game, plumes of smoke could be seen from the press box, rising beyond the left-field roof. Sportswriters who called their offices were told what was happening. But as the long afternoon wore on, the people in the stands had no clue about the disaster that was unfolding less than two miles from where they sat.

Mickey Lolich started the first game and was in his typical midsummer funk. Lolich had a two-week National Guard obligation each year, and the time spent away from the team seemed to destroy his pitching rhythm. This time he went into the seventh with a 2–2 tie, but an outfield error pushed across the winning run for New York. Lolich's record fell to 5–12. In a few hours he would have a rifle slung across his back, patrolling the streets of the terrified city. But now he was simply distraught over losing his 10th straight game over the last two months.

The Tigers came back in Game 2 with a 7–3 win behind John Hiller in relief of Johnny Podres. One of the big hits was a home run by Willie Horton. In a few hours he too would be on the streets of the city, pleading with rioters to go home. They were past listening, though, even to a hero like Horton.

Michigan did not observe daylight saving time in 1967, and by the time the second game ended, it was already close to dusk. Some may have noticed that the approaching evening seemed to have a smoky quality to it, too. Still no announcement was made about the social upheaval down the road—except for the fact that certain bus lines would not be operating. And the music played on.

It wasn't until fans got back to their cars and saw smoke pouring across the Lodge Freeway that they realized something terrible was going on in Detroit.

The Tigers lost a half game in the standings with the doubleheader split. But they actually had lost much, much more. As fear-driven rumors raced through the area for weeks after the riots ended, attendance at the ballpark took a nosedive. Fans who had waited for years to watch the Tigers in a pennant race feared for

Detroit was literally ablaze with race riots as the Tigers and the Yankees played a doubleheader in 1967. Both teams were blissfully unaware of the turmoil raging out in the streets.

their safety, and, especially when night games were scheduled, they chose to stay home.

What was badly begun was poorly ended. The pennant race stumbled on, and after a late summer 9–2 run, the Tigers found themselves in first place on September 16 with a one-game lead over Boston and Minnesota.

Then the bullpen collapsed, the defense kicked away two games, Denny McLain sustained a mysterious foot injury, and two tailenders shut them out. Finally, as if even higher forces were conspiring against the Tigers, it started to rain.

On September 27 the top four teams were still just one and a half games apart, with the Tigers tied for third. Their season was scheduled to end with a four-game home series against California, which had fallen out of the race earlier in the month. But on Thursday it rained, and on Friday it rained some more. The Tigers were faced with back-to-back doubleheaders to end the season, a scrambled pitching rotation, and a very simple scenario. If they swept, they won the pennant. If they took three out of four, they would face Boston in a playoff. Anything less and they were eliminated.

Lolich had righted himself from his July woes and in these critical final weeks he pitched three straight shutouts. He won the Saturday opener 5–0, and the Tigers went into the eighth inning of the nightcap, leading 6–2. Then it all came unglued. Four relievers could not stop the Angels. In a six-run rally that featured Hank Aguirre throwing to the wrong base instead of getting an easy out at home, the Tigers blew the game.

Now it was really simple. They had to sweep on Sunday…or else. Joe Sparma managed to hold off the Angels in the opener, and McLain, making his great return, started Game 2. He was gone by the third, unable to hold a 3–1 lead. By the time California had stopped cuffing Denny and his successors, it was 8–3. Dick McAuliffe knocked in two runs in the seventh to cut into the lead, but going into the all-or-nothing ninth, it was still 8–5.

Even though these games meant the entire season, the crowd was still more than 10,000 short of capacity. It was a fair measure of how deeply fear had affected the fan base.

What happened next, however, remains embedded in the nightmares of every longtime Tigers fan. Detroit put its first two hitters on base, and the Angels brought in George Brunet to pitch. He was a journeyman left-hander who somehow, someway always managed to beat the Tigers. He had defeated them in the season opener, and manager Mayo Smith described it as "Joe Dokes jumped up." Now here was old Joe again at the end of the road.

Second and first, nobody out. The crowd was pleading for the big hit to tie it up. One fan leaped to the roof of the Detroit dugout and bowed his head in an attitude of impassioned prayer.

After getting a harmless fly ball for the first out, Brunet settled in to face McAuliffe. He was Detroit's leadoff man and a clutch hitter. Moreover, he almost never hit into double plays; he had only one this entire season.

Need more be said? McAuliffe banged into a double play, ending the game and the season for the Tigers. Listening to a radio transmission of the game 600 miles to the east, the Red Sox leaped to their feet and began a wild clubhouse celebration. It took longer for it all to sink in for the Tigers.

"We had all winter to think about it," said catcher Bill Freehan. "We were the best team and we had blown it, and we knew that we had blown it. I think every one of us resolved that it wouldn't happen again in 1968."

But the scars of the terrible summer of 1967 would never be completely erased in Detroit.

MEDWICK'S FRUIT SALAD (1934)

Emotions were running high at the World Series of 1934. The two teams, the Tigers and the St. Louis Cardinals' Gas House Gang, genuinely detested each other.

It was the last time both Series teams would have player/managers—Mickey Cochrane and Frank Frisch. The Cards also had some genuinely tough guys in their dugout—Leo Durocher, Joe Medwick, Pepper Martin. Dizzy Dean was no wall-flower, either.

They baited the Tigers, disparaging their pitchers, aiming slurs at Hank Greenberg, and bragging that the Dean brothers would win four games. The fans caught the mood and gave it back to the Cards at Navin Field. When Dean, used as a pinch runner, was hit in the head by a thrown ball, one Detroit paper famously ran a headline reading: "Dean's Head X-Ray Reveals Nothing."

So when the seventh game arrived, it was getting uglier by the minute.

Tommy Bridges had put the Tigers one game away from victory by winning Game 5, 3–1, in St. Louis. But Paul Dean, the younger and quieter member of the brother act, outpitched Schoolboy Rowe 4–3 in Detroit the next day. There were no days off back then. Despite the fact that the two cities were over 500 miles apart and the teams traveled by train, the seven games were played in seven days.

It would be Dizzy against Elden Auker, the submarining right-hander, in Game 7. Auker had won 15 that year and beaten the Cards in Game 4. But Dizzy watched him warm up, walked over to Cochrane, and said, "He won't do, Mickey. He won't do."

Unfortunately, he was right. Auker couldn't make it past the third, and the big rally was touched off by a Dean double. Frisch

WATCH OUT FOR WILLIE

When a brawl broke out on the field, the Tigers would first look to see where Willie Horton was and then get out of the way. No one wanted to mess with him. The strangest incident in which he was involved came on June 11, 1975, when he objected to an inside pitch thrown by California's Frank Tanana.

Horton charged the mound and was ejected, but fights kept breaking out after he went to the locker room. Hearing the news on the radio, Horton came racing out in his undershirt and stocking feet to get in some more licks. He then started the second game of the doubleheader and got in two more hits—with his bat, that is. "I'm a family man," he said, by way of explanation.

then doubled with the bases loaded, Auker was out of the game, and the rout was on. By the time the inning was finished, St. Louis had scored seven runs. It was over, and everyone knew it was over.

The papers reminded Detroiters that the last time the Tigers had played a Game 7 (in 1909), Pittsburgh had mauled them 8–0. This looked like it might even be worse.

In the St. Louis sixth, Medwick slammed a two-out triple and went hard into third, spiking Marv Owen in the leg. Medwick claimed Owen tried to dupe him into thinking he had the ball and that a slide was the only way to get in. Whatever it was, the two men went face to face and had to be pulled apart. At the end of the inning it was 9–0.

Medwick trotted out to left field for the bottom half of the inning. This is where the Navin Field bleachers were located, and the occupants of the cheap seats were in a bad mood. The Series was lost and the hated Cards were beating up on the home team.

In those days, fans were allowed to bring their own treats into the ballpark. Many of the bleacherites had packed lunches. The uneaten portion of those meals now landed on Medwick.

Every imaginable kind of fruit and vegetable came soaring out of the stands, along with rolled-up newspapers and scorecards. Medwick moved closer to the infield and waited for the barrage to end. When it did and he returned to his normal position, the fans started again with renewed intensity.

"I never could figure out where all that produce was coming from," said Charlie Gehringer. "You'd have thought those lunches would have already been eaten. It was as if they had trucks coming up to the left-field stands to deliver more stuff."

Paul Gallico, the future best-selling novelist, was then a sportswriter with the *New York Daily News*. This is how he described the scene:

> "The dizziest, maddest, and wildest...World Series was interrupted by one of the wildest riots ever seen in a ballpark. For the first time I know of, the crowd forced a manager to remove a player from the field. Twenty thousand people, massed aslant in the left-field bleachers, turned into a deadly and vicious mob. Only a barrier of a steel screen and locked gates prevented them from pouring onto the field and mobbing outfielder Joe Medwick, who bears the innocuous nickname Ducky Wucky."

Maybe "deadly" is a bit strong, unless you believe in the Monty Python routine about how to defend yourself from an attack by a man armed with a fresh vegetable. Nevertheless, after watching several minutes of this scene, Commissioner Kenesaw M. Landis motioned Frisch to his box and told him that Medwick had to leave the game.

Frisch was furious, insisting his player had done nothing to provoke this. He demanded to know why. "Because I said so," said Landis, and that settled that.

The Cards finished laying on their 11–0 whupping, and the Series was over. It was the last hurrah for the Gas House Gang. The Tigers returned the next year and finally won their championship.

Medwick was traded to Brooklyn in 1940, managed by his old teammate, Durocher. In the sixth game with his new team he received a farewell token. He was beaned by a St. Louis pitcher and was never quite the same hitter again.

The incident was investigated by the Brooklyn district attorney's office. It concluded it was just the way old Gas Housers preferred to play the game.

DIAMOND MAYHEM (1909)

They played the game for keeps a century ago. It was not a pastime for gentle souls on the major league level. Intimidation was the order of the day, and if blood was spilled, that was the accepted price.

There were no guaranteed contracts and no one was getting rich on a ballplayer's salary. It often came down to a Darwinian struggle for survival.

Even by those standards, the World Series of 1909 was a brutal affair. The country's fans chose sides. Most of them backed Pittsburgh, with the great Honus Wagner at shortstop. Not many outside of Detroit cheered for the Tigers and the despised Ty Cobb.

In many respects it was a distant echo of the emotions that were in play when the Detroit Pistons of the Bad Boys era met the Chicago Bulls of Michael Jordan—only much meaner.

One of the Pirates' starting pitchers, Howie Camnitz, was weakened with a severe throat infection. Pittsburgh needed someone to step up in his place and took a gamble on a 27-year-old rookie, Babe Adams. He stopped the big Detroit hitters, Cobb and Sam Crawford, twice in this Series, but the Pirates were not eager to try him again in a seventh game. They wanted to end it in six. They wanted it badly.

The tone had been set when Wagner tagged Cobb in the mouth on an attempted steal of second in an earlier game. The Tigers star left the field with blood flowing from the wound. Some accounts say that Cobb had called out his intention to steal before the pitch and Wagner was just putting him in his place. Cobb denied it in later years, but it isn't altogether implausible.

The Tigers overcame an early 3–0 deficit in Game 6, and going into the ninth inning they were leading 5–3. This was a historic moment. This was the fifth World Series set for the best-of-seven games. None had gone the distance before, and there had been no

Despite his easygoing smile in this photo, Ty Cobb was generally disliked and had fierce battles with many opposing players. Photo courtesy of Getty Images.

provision for such an event this time either. Each city had hosted three of the games, and it was decided that the site of a seventh game would be decided by a coin flip. The teams had alternated wins through five games, but the Pirates didn't want to leave anything to chance. They set out to end it at Bennett Park.

George Mullin, the Tigers' top winner at 29–8, got the start, and after a rough first inning he stopped Pittsburgh cold. But the first two hitters in the Pirates ninth singled, and now the tying run was on base.

Detroit had overhauled its entire infield during the off-season and, incredibly, still repeated as pennant winners. Defensive lapses had killed them against the Cubs in the previous two Series. This time would be different. Tom Jones at first and George Moriarty at third were defensive specialists, while Jim Delahanty and Donie Bush gave them strength up the middle. In this inning they would all be tested as never before.

TY VERSUS THE BABE

The ugliest fight in Detroit's history came when Ty Cobb, who hated Babe Ruth and was convinced he was partly black, hollered a racial slur at him during a game at Navin Field in 1924. After two Yankees subsequently were plunked by pitches, both teams ran onto the field, and Ruth went right after Cobb. The fight spread to the stands, and after half an hour the game was awarded to New York on a forfeit.

Owen Wilson put down a bunt toward first, and when Jones went to touch the bag, he was knocked unconscious. The ball rolled away as a run scored and Bill Abstein raced to third. Jones had to be taken to the hospital, and the teams stood around snarling and threatening each other for 10 minutes. Crawford, a fairly inexperienced infielder, had to be moved in from center to play first. And the tying run was on third with no outs.

Moon Gibson deliberately slapped the ball toward Crawford, hoping the new first baseman would make a misplay in this critical situation. But Crawford fired the ball to the plate, and Abstein was tagged out.

He slid in with his spikes high, though, and cut catcher Charlie "Boss" Schmidt on the leg. The two men came up swinging at each other. Again it took several minutes for order to be restored before Schmidt, with blood oozing through his stocking, settled in again to catch. It was a terrible blunder by Abstein to get thrown out at the plate with the tying run and no one out, and the Pirates waived him right after the Series.

The two violent plays only seemed to heighten Pittsburgh's rage. As a pinch-hitter struck out, Wilson took off to steal third. He had already knocked Jones out of the game, and now he was down for double with Moriarty.

The injured Schmidt was able to get the ball to third in time, and Wilson ripped Moriarty's leg to shreds on the tag. The enraged third baseman had to be pulled off Wilson and needed help to walk off the field.

The Tigers won 5–4 to force a Game 7, but in the space of half an inning three of their starters had been injured. It was one of the bloodiest chain of events in Series history.

The Tigers also won the coin toss and got home field for the seventh game, but it didn't make much difference. Jones started but was still woozy, and Moriarty had to leave the game with his injury. Adams turned in his third straight victory, stopping the Tigers easily, 8–0.

It was 25 years before Detroit got into the Series again. When it did, the result was the fruit barrage thrown at Joe Medwick and detailed earlier. But compared with the bloodletting of 1909, that was a day at the beach.

DISCO DEMOLITION NIGHT (1979)

Those who believe that sooner or later everything happens to the Tigers regard this as one of their prime exhibits. It was, at the very least, the only time a major league ballgame had to be postponed because fans stormed the field to blow up disco records.

On the list of historic but ill-conceived promotions, Disco Demolition Night has to rank right near the top. Moreover, the Tigers were simply innocent bystanders. All they did was show up at Comiskey Park in Chicago to play a twi-nighter with the White Sox in July 1979.

The games were fairly meaningless. Neither team was going anywhere that year. The Tigers had created a bit of a stir by hiring Sparky Anderson to manage the team in mid-June. But his young ballclub was still a few years away from being a contender.

The White Sox were not attracting good crowds at their aging facility on the South Side. So when a local radio station approached them with a neat promotional idea, they were willing to listen.

Actually, the chief instigator had strong Detroit ties. Radio personality Steve Dahl had worked in Motown for several years and was a fairly recent arrival in Chicago. He lost his new job, however, when the station switched to an all-disco format. He was quickly picked up by another local rock station, but Dahl thirsted for revenge.

This was the height of the disco era, when places like New York's Studio 54 were major celebrity hangouts and acts like Donna Summer and the Bee Gees ruled the pop charts. Dahl claimed to detect a welling tide of blue-collar anger in the American heartland over such a musical "perversion." His great idea was to give admission to the ballpark for 98¢ to anyone who brought in some disco records to be destroyed between games of the doubleheader.

It worked amazingly well. The official crowd count was almost at the park's capacity of 48,000. But those who witnessed the evening's events swore thousands more managed to get inside somehow. Many of them were ripped and ready to party.

The Tigers won the opener 4–1 in rather mundane fashion. A win in the nightcap would get them to .500, with a 44–44 record. They got the win, all right, but in a way no one could have anticipated.

The potential for trouble was already evident in the first game. The customers, many of whom appeared to be more attuned to "A Whiter Shade of Pale" than the White Sox, found that their disco records made excellent devices for flipping onto the playing field. The aroma that filtered through the stands also was more reminiscent of a rock concert than a ballgame.

Finally, it was time for Dahl to take the field for his demolition. He walked to deep center with a box allegedly filled with disco records. It was undeniably rigged with an explosive charge. Dahl set it off, and the result was instant insanity.

The explosion itself tore a big hole in the outfield turf. But that was the least of the problems. The customers took Dahl's bomb as the signal to leap from the stands onto the field. They lit fires, destroyed a batting cage, tore up large chunks of grass, and generally ran amok.

Up in the Detroit TV broadcast booth, George Kell and Al Kaline, men who took the game of baseball seriously, were appalled. "I can't believe this can be happening in the United States of America," said Kell. The Tigers sat in the cramped visitors' locker room and watched in bemusement at what was going on just a few dozen yards away.

McAULIFFE ERUPTS

Dick McAuliffe was one of the mildest of individuals off the field. But between the lines he was a Tiger in temperament as well as uniform. When he felt Chicago's Tommy John had thrown at him deliberately in August 1968, he charged the mound.

John came out to meet him, McAuliffe rammed into his shoulder, and the pitcher went down with a season-ending injury. It was an ugly brawl that resulted in a five-game suspension for McAuliffe. The Tigers lost four of those games and narrowly escaped disaster in the pennant race.

White Sox officials urged the fans to leave the field. That didn't go over well. Eventually the police had to be called in from the local precinct, and after 39 arrests and six minor injuries, something close to order was reestablished.

Anderson walked out to inspect the field and pronounced it unplayable because his team would be risking injuries. The umpires agreed, and the game was forfeited to the Tigers. The next night was baseball as usual.

Dahl became a radio megastar in Chicago after this event, credited with "hastening the demise of disco." Baseball, despite the fears of Kell, recovered and rocked on.

But fans in Detroit were hardly models of decorum through the years. There was the World Series riot of 1934. In the late '60s management had to close down portions of the right-field upper deck after a cherry bomb and other assorted missiles landed a few feet from Boston's Ken Harrelson.

An even rowdier uproar occurred in July 1960, when a late-inning drive by the Yankees' Bill Skowron was ruled a game-tying two-run homer. Spectators seated down the right-field line claimed that the ball had hooked foul. They registered their displeasure by throwing the back of a chair at right fielder Roger Maris and driving the New York bullpen to seek cover in the dugout because of a barrage of other items. After this incident, the bullpens down both foul lines were fitted with protective roofs.

The worst outburst of all came after the final game of the 1984 World Series. Swarms of Tigers fans who couldn't get into the park began massing outside in the last few innings. When Detroit clinched the Series, they began to party big time. The celebration culminated with thousands of fans being terrorized as they left the stadium and a city police car being tipped over and set afire.

News photos of the burning car surrounded by cavorting celebrants, dancing around the flames as if it were a sacrificial offering, appeared all across the country. It took Detroit years to recover from those ugly images.

JUST PLAIN WEIRD

STEALING HOME (1958, 1969)

It may be the most exciting play in baseball. Oh, maybe an inside-the-park grand slam would top it in terms of sheer chaotic action. But stealing home is among the game's gems—and increasingly rare in a power-conscious sport.

The Tigers have a mixed record in this regard. Possibly the most celebrated home-stealer in the game's history, George Moriarty, played for Detroit. But they have also been the victims in two of the most brazen thefts since the dead-ball era ended.

Vic Power was the first American Leaguer to steal home twice in the same game. And two Minnesota Twins stole home in the same inning against Mickey Lolich.

Power was an immensely talented player from Puerto Rico. His real name was either Pellot or Pove. But he decided that for the purposes of playing baseball, Power sounded better. It also sounded less Hispanic. The '50s were a time in which such ballplayers were not as readily accepted as they are today. Nor was every team eager to have a black player on their roster.

Power came up in the Yankees chain, but New York was among the last of the big-league teams—along with the Tigers and the Red Sox—to integrate. Even though he had been a promising star in the minors, they sent him off to the Philadelphia A's in 1953 in an inconsequential shuffling of players.

Power blossomed into a standout first baseman. Although sometimes accused of being a hot dog because of his preference for one-handed catches, he was a skilled defensive player, a dangerous hitter, and an edgy competitor. The A's sent him to Cleveland midway through the 1958 season in a trade that would have major consequences. Roger Maris was the player who went the other way, and the A's obligingly wrapped him up in a deal with the Yankees two years later.

But Power was an immediate hit on an Indians team that would contend for the pennant in another year. In 1958, though, both Cleveland and Detroit were scuffling around .500. On August 14 Power took it upon himself to liven things up. The Tigers had won the first two of a three-game series, and Cleveland was hanging on to an 8–7 lead in the eighth of this one. Power decided they needed an insurance run. He singled, went to second on an error, and got to third on a wild pitch by Bill Fischer.

Minnie Minoso was the next hitter and a good one. But Power couldn't wait. Calling out in Spanish for Minoso (who came from Cuba) to get out of the way, Power came roaring down the line and beat the tag from Tigers catcher Charlie Lau.

As it turned out, the stolen run was needed because Detroit battled back in the ninth to tie it 9–9 and send the game into extra innings.

STEALING FIRST

Germany Schaefer was a guy who didn't know when to stop. Or where. Schaefer, one of the oddballs of the game's early years, played second base for the Tigers from 1905 to 1909. On one famous occasion, he walked and stole second base. Then on the next pitch, according to Sam Crawford and other witnesses, "He let out a whoop and headed back to first, the only man ever to steal first base."

Schaefer claimed he was trying to confuse the catcher into a throwing error. But the tactic was quickly made illegal in the rulebook.

In the tenth Power figured things had gone far enough. Frank Lary was making a rare relief appearance for Detroit and he loaded the bases with two outs. Power was the lead runner, and Rocky Colavito, the team's top slugger, was at bat. The crowd was calling for a big hit from the local favorite, but Power had another agenda. Once more he took off for the plate, this time without benefit of a shouted warning. And once more he stole home, this time winning the game 10–9.

No one in the American League, not even Moriarty or Ty Cobb, had ever done that twice in one game. The oddest thing was, with that historic steal, Power had swiped his last base of the entire season, and finished with a total of only three. Maybe he had a heavy date that night.

The Minnesota duo of Cesar Tovar and Rod Carew improved on that feat in 1969, stealing home twice in the same inning. Their victim was Lolich, who was just coming off his sensational work in the previous year's World Series. The impetus from that performance propelled him to a strong 4–1 start, so when the Tigers got away to a 2–0 lead in the May 18 game at Minnesota, the Twins decided that drastic measures needed to be taken.

Tovar, a versatile player and pesky hitter as a leadoff man, started the third with a single. Lolich was adept at holding runners on. In the tension-filled seventh game of the Series he had picked off the two best Cardinals base runners, Lou Brock and Curt Flood, in the same inning. But this time Tovar danced off the bag and baited him into a mistake. Lolich balked, and the runner trotted to second.

He then stole third and Lolich, showing signs of being rattled, walked Carew.

This brought Harmon Killebrew to the plate, one of the most dangerous right-handed sluggers of his era and perennially the Twins' top RBI man. But Tovar and Carew were feeling chipper. They pulled off a double steal, with Carew beating Bill Freehan's throw to second and Tovar sliding home ahead of the return toss.

Now the Tigers were coming unglued. With Killebrew still batting, Carew took off for third and slid in safely. Carew was in his third season with the Twins and would win his first of seven batting titles that year. Later in his career he would be noted as a threat to steal. But he had stolen only 17 bases in his first two years in the majors, and the Tigers weren't prepared for this sort of pilferage.

Lolich eyed him as he bluffed, coming down the line. Surely he wouldn't be thinking of trying it again. But that was precisely his plan. Lolich's pitch to Killebrew came in high and wide, and Carew slid home safely. He had stolen three bases during the same at-bat, which is pretty much all the rules allow.

Lolich pulled himself together after this outburst and shut out the Twins the rest of the way as the Tigers romped in, 8–2. Still, it had been another negative Tigers milestone in stealing home.

On the other hand Moriarty had made his reputation by stealing home 11 times in one season for Detroit. He was the third baseman on the 1909 pennant-winning team and stole a total of 189 bases in six full seasons with the Tigers. But those 11 steals earned him a certain immortality.

An editorial writer at the *Detroit News* was so moved by his exploits that he crafted an exhortatory piece headlined "Don't Die on Third." It urged young men who had reached third base through the sacrifice of family and their own efforts to go for it on the final stretch. They had to emulate Moriarty and make it all the way home.

Henry Ford was so impressed with the article that he reprinted hundreds of thousands of copies in pamphlet form and distributed them all across the country. For a brief time Moriarty and his steals of home were nationally famous. But as the Tigers learned, those steals can work both ways.

VERY SMALL BALL (1951)

For baseball purists it was a mockery, one of the ugliest things they had ever seen on a big-league field. For Bill Veeck it was the capper of a career filled with controversial promotions. He delighted in offending these purists.

For Tigers pitcher Bob Cain it was a ticket to trivia-game immortality, and the same could be said for Browns outfielder Frank Saucier.

But for Eddie Gaedel it was his great moment in the sun, and nothing he experienced in the remaining 10 years of his life could compare.

It was simply an accident of fate that the Tigers happened to be in town when Veeck sent a midget up to bat in the summer of 1951. The Browns were observing their 50th year in St. Louis, a run that had only two more seasons to go before they escaped to Baltimore and were transformed into the Orioles.

It was also the 50th anniversary of the Browns' radio sponsors, Falstaff Beer. Well, maybe. That date is in dispute, but Veeck, the team's owner, felt it was close enough. He also felt that he should do something absolutely spectacular to tie in the two anniversaries and give his fans a game to remember. Not that there were all that many fans to begin with. The Cardinals had long since eclipsed the Browns as the dominant team in the city. Sportsman's Park, the facility they shared, was often full for the Cards, a morgue for the Browns.

Veeck promised the ad reps at Falstaff that he would give them an absolutely incredible promotion for the Sunday doubleheader on August 19 with the Tigers. The Browns were dead last, as usual, and Detroit, a major disappointment that season, was in fifth place and fading.

Veeck promised everyone baseball clown Max Patkin, a salute to Falstaff, a jazz concert with Browns pitcher Satchel Paige playing the drums, and an even bigger surprise. The day before the big twin bill the feeble Browns smote the Tigers 20–9. All things considered, the crowd of more than 18,000, the largest in seven years for the Browns, had a lot to look forward to.

They got another Browns loss in the opener. Then they got their concert, and Patkin, and the salute to Falstaff between games. Veeck had a big, hollow birthday cake wheeled onto the field, and at the signal Gaedel popped out from inside. The 3'7" native of Chicago waved at everyone and then walked off the field.

That was it? That was the big surprise? The Falstaff people had been promised "spectacular," and all they got was a midget in a cake. They looked over at Veeck in the owner's box with disappointment leaning toward anger.

Whether you consider it a highlight or a lowlight, the moment when owner Bill Veeck of the St. Louis Browns sent a midget to bat against the Tigers has become indelible.

Veeck wanted to tell them what was coming next but he didn't dare. The whole stunt was being kept completely secret. Only Veeck, Gaedel, and manager Zack Taylor knew what was afoot. If anyone in authority had had an inkling, the whole thing would have been shot down in a flash. Veeck purposely had delayed wiring Gaedel's signed contract to the American League office until he knew everyone had left for the weekend. No one would see it until Monday morning, and by then it would be a fait accompli.

The Tigers went down in the first, and the crowd settled in to watch the Browns bat as the Falstaff people continued grumbling.

Saucier, playing in his only big-league season, was the leadoff man. Even he didn't know what was up. He played outfield in only three games all year and this was one of them. All he wanted to do was get up there and bat. Veeck said later that his only regret about the entire episode was the slight to Saucier.

Taylor called him back to the dugout, and out marched Gaedel as a pinch-hitter. As the crowd realized what was happening, they began to laugh and then applaud. Umpire Ed Hurley was not amused, however, and demanded to know what was going on. When Taylor showed him the valid contract, he had no alternative but to let Gaedel bat.

Veeck later indignantly denied that he had stolen the idea from a short story written by James Thurber in 1941, "You Could Look It Up." A midget batted in that tale, and it affected the outcome of a big game. Veeck said he had no such thing in mind, although it would have been nice. But if that had been his intent, he insisted, he might have sent Gaedel up late in the game with the bases loaded when it would have meant something. All he wanted to do was give the fans a good time.

Media coverage in Detroit was surprisingly subdued. The photograph of catcher Bob Swift on his knees to receive Cain's pitches, one of the most famous in baseball history, appeared on the sports page of the *Detroit News*, not on the front page as it surely would today. In fact, there was no reference at all to the incident on page one. Baseball writer Sam Greene treated it with good humor. "Veeck may try this on another day," he wrote. "He may try anything."

Only the editor who wrote the headline over the picture seemed upset. It read: "Funny? It Wouldn't Have Been If Wild Pitch Had Struck Him."

Swift said later that he thought of having Cain hit Gaedel, "but [he] didn't want to be charged with homicide."

Gaedel walked on four pitches, was taken out for a pinch-runner, and two days later was banned from the game by American League president Will Harridge as "not in the best interests of baseball." Harridge, in fact, banned all little people. Veeck responded that was fine with him and wondered if it applied to Yankees shortstop Phil Rizzuto, who was only 5'6".

Then he turned his attention to his next promotion, a lottery to choose the Browns' manager for a night.

THE SUNDAY KID (1959)

The season had started off about as dismally as any season in Detroit history. A team that was picked as a possible contender went 2–15. They lost a bone-chilling opening game when Chicago's Nellie Fox, who hadn't hit a homer in two years, drilled one to right in the fourteenth inning. From there on, it would get much, much worse.

The old baseball adage says, "When the bus breaks down, fire the driver." So manager Bill Norman, the minor league lifer who had been given the job one year before, was out, and veteran Jimmy Dykes was brought in on a salvage operation.

He showed up just in time to face the defending-champion Yankees in a Sunday doubleheader at Briggs Stadium. It really wasn't that bad of a team to inherit. Harvey Kuenn would win the batting title, Al Kaline was in the middle of the lineup, Jim Bunning and Frank Lary anchored the pitching staff. Eddie Yost, one of the great leadoff men of the era, was playing third base.

The starting left fielder was Charlie Maxwell. He had come over in a nothing trade with Baltimore a few years before and turned into a better-than-average hitter with the ability to reach the short right-field seats at the stadium frequently. Kuenn was down with an injury, so Dykes batted Maxwell third in the opener.

Radio announcer Van Patrick had taken to calling Maxwell "Old Paw Paw," after the small town in western Michigan. Actually, he hailed from nearby Lawton, but there wasn't anything funny about that name. So Paw Paw it was, and he was among the most popular Tigers with the fans.

He homered in the seventh inning of the opener off Don Larsen as the Tigers choked off their losing streak with a 4–2 win. Then in the nightcap Old Paw Paw went nuclear.

First inning, a two-run homer off another local boy, Yankees starter Duke Maas of Utica. (Nothing funny about that name either.)

CALAMARI CALAMITY

Matt Anderson was a promising relief pitcher for the Tigers. He threw hard but very straight and not always for strikes. To celebrate the Red Wings reaching the 2002 Stanley Cup finals, the Tigers held an octopus tossing contest—hearkening back to the ancient Detroit tradition of throwing these slimy creatures on the ice during the playoffs.

Anderson gave it his best heave…and ended up with an arm injury that ended his career. An octopus has eight arms. Somehow it seems there could have been one to spare for Matt.

Fourth inning, a three-run homer off Johnny Kucks. Seventh inning, a solo homer off Zack Monroe.

There was also a walk mixed in there, so in his last five times to the plate Maxwell had hit four homers. The Tigers won both games, and it was pretty good work for a Sunday afternoon.

Detroit proceeded to win five of their next six, and the following Sunday Maxwell creamed a three-run homer off Kansas City for another win.

"It's Old Paw Paw and his Sunday punch," exulted Patrick in the broadcast booth.

Then on the final Sunday of the month he came up with two on in the ninth in a tie game with Cleveland and he did it again. The Tigers won 7–4, and while the team still wasn't up to .500, the entire country was learning about Maxwell and Sundays.

On June 14 the Tigers went into Yankee Stadium for yet another Sunday doubleheader. All of his previous Sunday homers were hit in Detroit. But since Maxwell's initial barrage, the Tigers had gone 28–12 and were now just two games out of first.

Whitey Ford was starting for the Yankees, though, and into the eighth of the opener he had Detroit baffled, 2–0. Then Yost singled, Kuenn singled, and Maxwell sliced a three-run homer off the left-field foul pole. It was his seventh Sunday homer of the year, and the New York media were all over the story. Even though the best he could do in the nightcap was a double, the Tigers swept, and the legend was made.

Unfortunately, legends can't change hard facts. That was the pinnacle for the Tigers. They immediately went into another slump and fell permanently out of the race. Maxwell hit another four Sunday homers, but never delivered in quite such dramatic fashion again.

The record shows that he finished with 31 home runs in 1959, his most productive year in the majors. But the fans who were around then know the number doesn't begin to capture the drama of Old Paw Paw coming to the plate on Sunday.

LET'S PLAY TWO AND A HALF (1962)

On the long list of New York Yankees sluggers who broke the hearts of Tigers fans, the name Jack Reed does not figure very high. Nor should it. He only was around for parts of three seasons and came to bat all of 129 times.

But he ended one of the longest and strangest games in Detroit history. In terms of innings, the game fell two short of the all-time Tigers record of 24. In terms of length, however, it went on just this side of forever—seven hours on the button before a decision was reached. Fans who started the day sweltering in the

THREE FOR NEUN

Johnny Neun didn't play with the Tigers for long, just 272 games in parts of four seasons. But in 1927 he did something no other Detroit player has matched. Neun pulled off an unassisted triple play.

What made it even more unusual is that he played first base. Only one other player at that position has ever done it. In a game against Cleveland on May 31, with runners at first and second, Neun backhanded a liner going to his right, tagged the runner trying to get back to first, and his momentum carried him to second before that runner could return.

sun ended it shivering in the evening chill. It was a record at the time, but was eclipsed by 25 minutes just two years later.

Nonetheless, the 9–7 loss on June 23, 1962, was the longest game ever played at Tiger Stadium. One of the most unexpected, too, because after three innings it seemed the hitters were solidly in control. Both starters had long since departed the premises, and the Yankees led 7–6.

Frank Lary, who usually dominated the Yankees, and Bob Turley were the opposing pitchers. But Lary was trying unsuccessfully to come back from an injury he had suffered in the home opener while legging out a triple against the Yanks. Turley, the pitching star of the 1958 World Series, had been bothered by arm troubles ever since and was in his final season with New York.

So when the Yanks pounded their old nemesis for six runs in the first, including a three-run homer by light-hitting Clete Boyer (so poorly regarded as a hitter that former manager Casey Stengel once pinch hit for him in the second inning of a Series game), it looked like a long afternoon for Tigers fans. They didn't know the half of it.

Purnal Goldy, a spring-training sensation, followed with a surprise three-run shot of his own in the Detroit first, and Turley was gone. The Yanks added a final run off Lary in the second to make it 7–3. But the Tigers moved to within a run in the third with another surprise clutch hit, this one a two-run double by reserve catcher Mike Roarke, who was a .230 lifetime hitter. So there was a pattern emerging in this game. Big offense was coming from where you'd least expect it.

In the Tigers' sixth, the tie was finally forged when Billy Bruton singled, stole second, and came home on a Rocky Colavito single. No one could have guessed that would be all the scoring there would be for the next 16 innings.

The Yankees would get 20 hits and the Tigers 19. The Yankees would leave 21 runners on base, the Tigers 22. The two teams would use 14 pitchers and a total of 43 players. The Tigers were reduced to sending up pitcher Don Mossi, a career .163 hitter, as a pinch-hitter. Colavito wound up with seven hits in the game.

Time after time, though, the bullpens turned away each threat. Jim Bouton, then a 23-year-old rookie, came on in the sixteenth and blanked Detroit on three hits the rest of the way. Preceding him, Tex Clevenger and Bud Daley threw shutout ball for nine innings.

After Lary's departure, a committee of five Detroit relievers stopped the Yankees for 19 scoreless innings, with Terry Fox working eight of them.

The Tigers had just missed a pennant the previous year and were challenging again. But Al Kaline had gone down with a fractured collarbone while making a game-saving catch at Yankee Stadium and Detroit was fading fast. The Tigers were three and a half games out of the lead and desperately needed this game.

The Tigers actually loaded the bases with none out in the eleventh on a Colavito triple and two walks. But after one out, Dick Brown bunted into a double play on a suicide squeeze when he popped the ball to the catcher.

The teams were then only halfway through this long, strange trip. But the man who would end it was ready to come in. Reed entered the affair in the thirteenth inning, the third right-field manager Ralph Houk used. He had gone zero for three by the time Detroit's seventh pitcher, Phil Regan, took up the battle in the twenty-second.

Regan walked Roger Maris, always a threat to break up a ballgame, with one out and turned his attention to Reed. He was in his second season and used primarily as a defensive replacement for the slowing Mickey Mantle. He had shown scant long-ball power, and Regan felt he could work on him with some confidence. But Reed provided the final surprise of the day, a two-run shot over the 365-foot sign in left field. Colavito's last hit of the game was all the Tigers had left, and the longest day was over.

The Tigers had a history of important games that went long, but both of the others ended in no-decisions and also figured in a pennant race.

In 1907 the Tigers were on a vital late-September eastern swing and had to play two in Philadelphia. The A's were just half a game behind Detroit when Wild Bill Donovan beat them in the opener of the series. After two days of rain, Donovan, who would go 25–4 that year, was sent out again. This time he didn't have it.

The A's jumped him for a 7–1 lead, and it appeared that the Tigers would leave town half a game in front again with a full week left to play. But just as in 1962, the Tigers fought back. They tied it, 8–8, when Ty Cobb ripped a two-run ninth-inning homer off Hall of Famer Rube Waddell. According to legend, Connie Mack was so stunned by the blast that he slid off the end of the dugout bench and into the bat rack.

It got even crazier, though. The teams traded runs in the tenth, and then the A's slugging first baseman, Harry Davis, sent a long fly to center. Sam Crawford was about to make the catch in front of the roped-in overflow crowd when two Philadelphia policemen emerged from the gallery and knocked him down. The umpires ruled that Davis was out due to fan interference, which touched off a brawl that poured onto the field and into the stands, with the Tigers fighting the cops at one point.

After that interruption, the teams struggled on to a 9–9 tie that finally was called because of darkness after 17 weary innings. Detroit had protected its precious half-game margin, and that's how the race ended. Because of rainouts and this tie, the A's only played 145 games and the Tigers 150—well short of the full 154-game schedule. If the games had been made up, Philly might still have had a chance. But in 1907 travel was by train. Teams couldn't jet from town to town, and scheduling on short notice was next to impossible. So the results stood, and the Tigers had their first pennant, thanks in part to this tie. (The same sort of thing happened the following year, when the Tigers edged Cleveland by half a game by playing one fewer game than their rivals.)

Detroit's longest game came in another pennant-winning year, 1945. It was also played in Philadelphia, although things were a lot calmer than they had been 38 years before. It ended 1–1 when darkness set in after 24 innings.

The game was distinguished chiefly by pitcher Les Mueller's heroic pitching performance. He went 19⅔ innings without a decision. It was Mueller's only season with the Tigers, and his long stint amounted to one-seventh of the total innings he would pitch all year. Since the Tigers won the pennant by just one and a half games, the long tie was a factor in this race, too.

TEAMMATES

COBB AND KALINE: FIRE AND ICE (1905–1927, 1953–1975)

In a book titled *The Good, the Bad, and the Ugly,* it's hard to find a category that best describes Tyrus Raymond Cobb. He fits all three.

He was assuredly the greatest player in Tigers history, and some would argue in all of baseball. But he was hated by nearly everyone in the game, including most of his own teammates. He was also an unapologetic racist and capable of some of the ugliest actions imaginable, including going into the stands in New York and punching a fan in a wheelchair who was heckling him.

The man who shares virtually every record in the Tigers book with him had the opposite persona. Al Kaline played with a quiet grace to which statistics can't quite do justice. Almost imperturbable on the field, he was a leader by example instead of rhetoric in the clubhouse.

One of Kaline's favorite expressions was "You can't play this game afraid." But Cobb's goal was to put fear into everyone he played against. When Kaline was knocked down by a pitch, he would get up quickly, dig in again with a slight glare at the pitcher, and lace a hit somewhere. When Cobb was low-bridged, he would usually bunt down the first-base line, make the pitcher cover the bag, and try to knock him into the first row of the boxes. That's how their separate greatness was defined.

Even in the era before sports talk radio and ESPN shaped the agenda, Cobb's attitude and take-no-prisoners demeanor made him baseball's bad guy all over the country. In the 1909 World Series almost everyone rooted for Pittsburgh because they wanted to see veteran star Honus Wagner show Cobb up—which he did.

Maybe the epitome of Cobb hatred occurred the following year, when he was involved in a close race for the batting title with Cleveland's Nap Lajoie. The prize was a brand-new Chalmers automobile. Lajoie was 36 years old and as widely admired as Cobb was detested. He played second base with consummate skill and was an artist with the bat.

The two were just a few points apart heading into the final weekend. Cobb developed an eye inflammation that caused him to sit out the last two games, although there were some who said he really had his eye on that new car. He was just 23 and already had three straight batting titles to his credit. The St. Louis Browns decided they would end that streak and give the title to Lajoie.

In a meaningless season-ending doubleheader, manager Jack O'Connor told his third baseman to play back on the grass, enabling Lajoie to bunt repeatedly for hits. He beat out seven of

Though they might have been as different as yin and yang, Al Kaline (pictured here) and Ty Cobb share twin billing at the top of many Detroit Tigers club records. Photo courtesy of Getty Images.

them, added a triple, and went eight-for-nine on that day. Lajoie finished at .384, but Cobb beat him out by less than one point.

The ensuing scandal caused an uproar. Several of the Tigers reportedly sent a congratulatory telegram to Lajoie, under the mistaken idea that he had won. Sportswriters fulminated, but mostly came down on the side of the hated Cobb. O'Connor was banished from the league by baseball officials. Chalmers, loving all the publicity, decided to award cars to both men.

"Why do they so resent Cobb when he plays the game at every point on the field, giving his best at every moment, and makes life miserable for those less willing," wrote New York columnist Heywood Broun. "Hated why? What player gives the fans so much value for their money?"

Cobb went on to win eight more batting titles. He grew rich investing in the young Detroit auto industry and Coca-Cola in his home state of Georgia. The hatred ran right off his back.

Cobb was 18 when he played his first game with Detroit, and he was a batting champion at 20. Kaline's birthday was one day later than Cobb's, and he followed the same career track exactly.

The game had changed a lot, however, in the 48 years that separated their arrivals in Detroit. Kaline never regarded himself as a power hitter, but still finished with 399 homers. No Tiger hit more. Cobb dominates most other offensive categories, but it was on defense that Kaline truly shone. He could turn games around with his glove.

"Used to be a ball was hit to the right-field corner and I knew it was a hit," said Casey Stengel after watching Kaline perform against his Yankees. "With that young feller out there now, I have to get up off my seat in the dugout and make sure."

In his first full season, the Tigers removed the box seats in that section of Briggs Stadium to give Kaline more room to track down batted balls. It was always known thereafter as "Kaline's Corner."

His unerring throws, sense of timing, and the jump he got on a ball made Kaline the greatest right fielder of his era, and maybe of all time. It was a shock to see him make a mistake.

Kaline himself relished the memory of the leaping grab he made of a Mickey Mantle home-run bid at Yankee Stadium. "The New York

FANNING THE BREEZE

There have been some big swingers who often missed the pitch in Detroit. But the team's all-time strikeout leader was primarily a leadoff man. Lou Whitaker had 1,099 in his career, which was 18 more than Norm Cash. Al Kaline, who played in more games than any other Tiger, finished third with 1,020.

broadcasters never saw it in my glove," he said, "and they went off the air saying that it was a home run and the Yankees had won the game."

It was another fearless catch at that field, however, that marked a watershed in Kaline's career. He was on pace to hit 40 home runs in the 1962 season, and the Tigers had hopes of contending with the Yankees for a second straight year. They went into New York in late May for a series that they felt would set the tone.

With Hank Aguirre protecting a 2–1 lead in the ninth, the Yankees put the tying run on with two outs. Elston Howard then sent a sinking liner to right. It looked like a sure game-tying hit. Kaline came swooping in, though, and caught the ball just before it hit the ground. That ended the game. It also ended Kaline for the next two months. He broke his collarbone on the play.

"We won the game and lost the season," Aguirre mourned later.

Kaline was just 27 when he was injured, and while he maintained a high standard of performance afterward, it was never quite the same sustained level as before. One injury after another afflicted him: A beaning. A broken hand. A childhood malady that affected his toes and became more painful with the passing years.

Only twice more was he able to come to bat more than 500 times in a season. He hit .300 over a full season only two more times. His career average before that injury was .308; afterward it was only .287. Even factoring in the effects of aging, that is quite a drop-off.

Kaline did have something that Cobb never attained—a World Series championship ring. While Cobb's Tigers lost three

Series in a row, and he was regarded as a major disappointment in two of them, Kaline was one of the hitting stars of the 1968 champions.

Cobb also managed the Tigers for six rather forgettable seasons in the 1920s, and successfully maintained his record of being hated by nearly everyone he came in contact with. Kaline, who never spent a day in the minors and never wore another uniform in his entire professional career, never got that job.

"It was never offered to me, and I didn't want to put the Tigers organization in the position of having to say 'no' if I asked for it," he said later.

Besides, great managers usually have to come down somewhere between fire and ice.

DIZ AND HOOT'S EXCELLENT ADVENTURE (1950)

The Yankees were in town. The Tigers were in the race. It was a night game at Briggs Stadium back when night games there were still a rarity, limited to about a dozen a season.

The combination was irresistible, and many of the 51,000 fans who packed the ballpark on that warm June night in 1950 swore it was the greatest game they ever saw.

The Tigers came back not once but twice, and the two teams set a record by hitting 11 home runs in the game. But the final one took it all, and it never even left the field.

Pitcher Dizzy Trout brought the Tigers back with the unlikeliest hit of his career, and the winner came off the bat of left fielder Hoot Evers. This was his greatest season in the majors. He led the league in triples, put together a 19-game hitting streak, and made the All-Star team. But at the end of the day it wasn't enough, as the Yankees won their second of five straight pennants. Still, in this game Trout and Evers made their fans believe that anything was possible.

This was Detroit's best team since the wartime winners of 1945. Only pitchers Hal Newhouser, Trout, and catcher Bob Swift remained from that bunch. But the new cast was an impressive group.

The Tigers had traded for future Hall of Famer George Kell, and he had blossomed into a batting champion. The farm system sent up an entire outfield—Evers, Johnny Groth, and Vic Wertz. Other trades brought in the right side of the infield, second baseman Jerry Priddy and first baseman Don Kolloway. Veteran

Dizzy Trout (center) and Hal Newhouser (right) talk with a reporter in the clubhouse after a game in 1950. Photo courtesy of Getty Images.

Fred Hutchinson and youngsters Art Houtteman and Ted Gray completed the starting rotation.

The only downer was the loss of Virgil Trucks. Detroit's top winner the previous year, Trucks went down with a back injury seven games into his season. That was a hole the Tigers struggled to fill.

They were unmistakably contenders, though, and by mid-June they were 22 games over the .500 mark. Even three straight losses in Washington couldn't detract from the anticipation of this four-game home set with the Yankees. The Tigers were still one game ahead going into the opener. Manager Red Rolfe, an old Yankee himself from the four-time champions of the late 1930s, decided to go with Gray as the first game starter.

Kell described Rolfe as a rather austere man who didn't communicate well with his players. This was his first managing job in the majors, but his chilly personality hadn't become a problem yet. After all, the Tigers were winning.

It was apparent, however, that Gray was not up to the job. The Yankees pounded him early and often and raced off to a 6–0 lead. Rolfe had to pull him. His surprising choice as a replacement was Trout.

Diz had just started and lost the previous day in Washington. He wasn't a young man anymore. In six more days he would be 35 and no longer the pitcher who had racked up 352 innings and won 27 games in 1944. In the previous year Rolfe had turned him into strictly a relief man, and it hadn't worked out well. Trout was unhappy with the shift and largely ineffective. But when Trucks went down, Trout was only too ready to take his spot in the rotation.

Tommy Byrne was on the mound for the Yankees, a left-hander with severe control problems. Still, he had won 15 the previous year and seemed able to protect this six-run lead.

But his collapse was sudden and violent. With one out, Byrne gave up singles to Groth and Kolloway and a walk to Bob Swift. It was Trout's turn to bat with the bases loaded. Diz was a better than fair hitter for a pitcher, so Rolfe had no qualms about letting him hit in this situation.

His lifetime average was .213, and in every season between 1942 and 1952 he hit at least one homer. In his biggest year he hit five of them. None, however, were bigger than this one.

Trout's grand slam into the left-field seats cut the Yankees' lead to just two runs. One out later, Priddy knocked Byrne out of the game with a home run, and it was 6–5. The Yankees brought in Fred Sanford, who surrendered a single to Kell before Vic Wertz gave the Tigers the lead with a tremendous home run to right-center field. Evers followed with another shot, and the Tigers had scored eight times and were now in front. But the Yankees were not through. They already had five homers—two by Hank Bauer and others by Joe DiMaggio, Yogi Berra, and Jerry Coleman. When pinch-hitter Tommy Henrich connected in the eighth, New York was back out front, 9–8.

Joe Page was a closer before anyone knew about closers or saves. When historians went back and figured out the stats for relief pitchers in the pre-save era, Page was *the* guy in the late 1940s. He had had 60 of them for the Yankees in the previous three seasons, and this was at a time when starters were expected to finish what they began. Henrich got the nickname "Old Reliable" for hitting in the clutch, and in his own niche Page was just as reliable.

But the left-hander was in his last year with the Yankees. Although manager Casey Stengel didn't realize it yet, he was not the same closer. By the end of the year, Tom Ferrick was splitting the job with him.

This proved to be one of the times Page faltered. With one man on in the last of the ninth, Evers came to bat. The "Hoot" nickname came from his mother, who was extremely fond of Hollywood cowboy movie hero Hoot Gibson. A college star at the University of Illinois, Evers was now 29. He had lost five critical years to World War II, but for the last three seasons he had been one of the rocks in the Tigers' lineup. Never a big home-run hitter, he would still drive in 103 runs that season.

Evers sent Page's pitch on a line to right-center. Briggs Stadium was renowned as a slugger's paradise, with its overhanging second deck in a short right field and its friendly power alleys. Consequently, it was hard to hit an inside-the-park homer here unless it somehow got into dead center. The wall in that area was 440 feet away from home plate, one of the deepest in the majors, and there was also a flagpole in play to complicate things.

DiMaggio was, of course, one of the greatest defensive outfielders of all time. But this time the ball caromed off the wall away from him and rolled into the deepest recess of the field. As Evers raced around the bases, the huge crowd screamed. Third-base coach Dick Bartell took the chance and waved Evers in to go for the win. He scored easily, and the Tigers won 10–9. It was only the eighth inside-the-park homer in the history of the ballpark.

Detroit also took two of the next three, but a late-season New York surge overtook them. You couldn't beat the Yankees for keeps in those years. But for one night, it was great.

AROUND THE KEYSTONE (1977–1995)

It wasn't supposed to happen in the era of "when's the next plane out of town" free agency. Stars rarely stayed put. There was always a better offer coming in from somewhere.

The days when Al Kaline could spend an entire career wearing no other uniform but the Tigers' were as long gone as an Ernie Harwell home-run call.

For two such players to stay together for an extended length of time was almost beyond comprehension. So the 1,918 games that Alan Trammell and Lou Whitaker spent together in the middle of the Detroit infield beat all the odds.

It was not only the longest tenure for a double play combination in the history of baseball. It was also the longest streak of togetherness ever in the American League. (The Cubs' Billy Williams and Ron Santo, playing far less demanding positions, hold the major league mark with 2,015 games.)

Only Al Kaline and Ty Cobb played more games with the Tigers than Whitaker, and Trammell holds fifth place. After all those games and all those times at bat, when the two of them finished, Whitaker had just four more hits in his career than Trammell.

They came through the Tigers farm system together, the shy kid from Brooklyn and the quietly aggressive one from San Diego.

LOLICH MOWS 'EM DOWN

On the other end of the stat sheet, Mickey Lolich struck out more opposing hitters than any other Detroit pitcher, with 2,679. A distant second was Jack Morris, with 1,980.

Lolich also gave up more homers than anyone else. His 329 were eight more than Morris's. He also leads everyone with 39 shutouts, five more than dead-ball–era star George Mullin. When it comes to wins, though, Lolich, at 207, trails Mullin by two and all-time leader Hooks Dauss, who had 222 with the Tigers.

From opposite ends of the country they met at second base and gave the Tigers the best middle infield in the game for most of two decades.

The Tigers were in one of their spells of aimlessness throughout the middle '70s. A lot of talent passed through the gates of Tiger Stadium after the breakup of the 1968 champions, including Mark Fidrych, Ron LeFlore, Jason Thompson, Steve Kemp, Rusty Staub. They made the All-Star teams, but somehow the team never added up to a contender. They simply had no strength up the middle, where pennants are won and lost.

In 1977 the Tigers' middle infield consisted of second baseman Tito Fuentes, who led the league in errors, and shortstop Tom Veryzer, who hit .197. That team finished 14 games under .500, the fourth straight losing season under manager Ralph Houk.

Houk was brought in because of his reputation for patience with young players. But the Tigers were trying everyone's patience. They seemed stuck on stagnant.

Trammell and Whitaker were called up from the minors together in September. Houk started them both in the second game of a doubleheader on September 9. In their dual debut, Whitaker got three hits, Trammell two, and away they went.

They stayed in the lineup for the last few weeks of the season, and there was no question about who the starters at second and short would be for 1978. It was automatic.

Suddenly, the Tigers had a pulse. They got off to one of their strongest starts in years and were actually in first place in the middle of May. That didn't last. Even so, they finished with 86 wins, a 12-game improvement over the previous year. The new infield was not incidental to these developments.

The two rookies were still contact hitters. Combined, they hit a total of five home runs. But their moves around the bag were something Detroit fans hadn't seen for years—they had to ransack their memories, go all the way back to Charlie Gehringer and Billy Rogell in the 1930s, to find a comparison.

"People took it for granted after a while that Lou and I worked that smoothly," said Trammell. "What they didn't see was the hundreds of repetitions in infield drill every day. We knew instinctively where the other was going to be in every situation and soon we didn't even have to look. But it wasn't magic. It was work."

It took several more years before all the pieces were in place. Lance Parrish joined the Tigers that same year to become the regular catcher and Jack Morris broke in on the pitching staff.

By 1984 the two infielders were the heart and nerve of the team. Whitaker was a leadoff man with power, a .289 hitter with 13 homers. The slap-hitting Trammell was now a deadly number-two hitter, able to drive the ball with power to all fields. He hit .314, added 14 homers, and was the MVP of the World Series.

The two of them stayed on for another 11 years after that, never winning another championship but continuing to demonstrate how the infield should be played. Whitaker retired after the 1995 season. The Tigers finished that desultory campaign with an extended road trip, so their final game together was in Baltimore. Just for old times' sake, Sparky Anderson batted Whitaker leadoff and Trammell second. They were pulled after one time at bat, although Trammell got one of Detroit's two hits in the game off Mike Mussina.

Trammell decided to remain for one more year. But the magic had flown. Second base was being played by some guy named Mark Lewis, the Tigers once again sank to last place, and the party was truly over. But the honored guests had stayed for a long, long time.

SLUG AND ASSOCIATES (1921–1927)

Hitting .380 for an entire season is a rather splendid achievement. Since 1941, when Ted Williams became the last man to bat over .400, only four players have managed to finish the year at that level—Williams again, Tony Gwynn, Rod Carew, and George Brett.

But over the course of seven years in the 1920s, the standard season for Harry Heilmann was .380. He won batting championships in every odd-numbered year of that decade between 1921 and 1927. His batting averages for those years were .394, .403, .393, and .398.

Since the end of the dead-ball era, Heilmann and Rogers Hornsby are the only two right-handed hitters to hit .400 in a season. The reasons for that are obvious. Lefties have an innate advantage in that they are closer to first base and moving toward it when they finish their swing. They also face a preponderance of right-handed pitching. Righties get no such favors. Heilmann was also a heavy-legged runner. He got few infield hits—almost everything he hit was a line drive.

Very few franchises have ever assembled the sort of hitting power that was routinely arrayed across the Detroit outfield in that era. Out of the 21 American League batting championships that could be won between the years 1907 and 1927, the Tigers took 17. Most of that was the work of 12-time champion Ty Cobb, but Heilmann had his odd four, and Heinie Manush won in 1926 when Heilmann "slumped" all the way to .367.

In fact, every Detroit outfielder hit at least .367 that year. Bob Fothergill, nicknamed "Fats" because his 230 pounds were packed onto a 5'10" frame, was the third man in the picture. He never hit under .300 in eight years with the Tigers and has the distinction of being the last man ever to pinch hit for Cobb. Not since the 1890s had an entire outfield exceeded that batting mark. Despite it all, the Tigers finished sixth in the standings.

Heilmann was the most cordial of Tigers, the polar opposite of the ferocious Cobb. When Cobb was named manager in 1921, he decided to concentrate his efforts on Heilmann, instructing him to use his wrists more, stand with his feet closer together, and shorten his swing. It was all the more remarkable because, when Cobb was a player, he had ignored Heilmann.

Heilmann responded to the expert tutelage and returned the favor by winning his first batting championship. The runner-up, who lost out by five points, was Cobb.

In 1925 Heilmann went into September trailing Tris Speaker by 50 points. In an incredible late-season surge, Heilmann overtook him on the last day and won by four points. He repeated the feat in 1927, refusing to sit out the final day of the year and winning his last batting crown, over Al Simmons.

The only year the Tigers were actually in the pennant race during that period, 1924, coincided with Heilmann's least productive season. All he did was hit .346, drive in 114 runs, score 107 more, and miss just one game. That was an off year for Heilmann.

The strain his batting style put on his wrists caught up with him, however, and from that time on he was never completely free of pain caused by advancing arthritis.

Although his relationship with Cobb was warmer than what Cobb had with anyone else on the team, Heilmann had a tough decision to make in 1925. One of the players Cobb had ticked off, pitcher Dutch Leonard, went to Heilmann when he was cut from the team and told him he had solid evidence that Cobb had bet on games.

He had letters from Cobb and Smoky Joe Wood, as well as Speaker, indicating that they had conspired to fix a game in 1919

THE FOUR *B* BOYS

During part of the 1958 season the Tigers had a rare double-play combination. The Bolling brothers, Frank and Milt, both started in the middle of the Detroit infield. The brother act only lasted 24 games, but it was a unique event in Tigers history.

When Ray Boone played first base that year and Reno Bertoia was at third, announcer Van Patrick nicknamed the infield group the "Four Busy Bees."

between the Tigers and the Indians. Since Cleveland was still in the race, and this was the same year as the infamous Black Sox World Series, these were serious charges.

Heilmann never hesitated. He went to team owner Frank Navin immediately, and the letters were turned over to the commissioner's office. While Cobb and Speaker were both threatened with expulsion, Leonard refused to testify against them in person, and the case fell apart.

Cobb never held it against Heilmann, though, and campaigned actively for his old teammate to be admitted to the Hall of Fame. Incredibly, that took 20 years after his retirement, and, unfortunately, one year after his death. Heilmann never played on a pennant-winning team, and that hurt his case, but it was still an incredible oversight by the admissions committee.

Or maybe its members didn't believe his numbers told the story.

NOTES

THE GOOD

"I said to the plate umpire...": Ritter, Lawrence S. *The Glory of Their Times: The Story of the Early Days of Baseball Told by the Men Who Played It* (New York: Macmillan Co., 1966), p. 260.

"Even if he broke back right away...": Cantor, George. *The Tigers of '68: Baseball's Last Real Champions* (Dallas, TX: Taylor Publishing Co., 1997), p. 203.

"He had just abused me in the past...": Cantor, George. *Wire to Wire: Inside the 1984 Detroit Tigers Championship Season* (Chicago: Triumph Books, 2004), p. 4.

"That was the most painful experience...": Cantor, George. *Out of Nowhere* (Chicago: Triumph Books, 2006).

"He was just overpowering that season...": Greenberg, Hank with Ira Berkow. *Hank Greenberg: The Story of My Life* (Chicago: Triumph Books, 2000).

"One Bobo told me...": Anonymous article. "Baseball's Marco Polo," *The Washington Post,* July 16, 1948.

"The fences were so short...": Cantor, George. *The Tigers of '68: Baseball's Last Real Champions* (Dallas, TX: Taylor Publishing Co., 1997), p. 188.

"I was never accepted by the black fans...": Valade, Jodie. "Ozzie Virgil: The Man Who Broke the Barrier," *The Detroit Free Press,* June 17, 1997, section D, p. 1.

THE BAD

"It's true I've never managed before...": Cantor, George. *Wire to Wire: Inside the 1984 Detroit Tigers Championship Season* (Chicago: Triumph Books, 2004), p. 137.

"Bartell must have thought he had no chance...": Falls, Joe. *The Detroit Tigers: An Illustrated History* (New York: Walker & Co., 1989), p. 96.

THE UGLY

"Charlie Gehringer, who was in the on-deck circle...": ibid., p. 54.

"I respected him as a manager...": Cantor, George. "My Three Sons Made the Calls," *The Detroit Free Press Magazine,* July 8, 1973, p. 16.

"I ran back to Barnett...": Cantor, George. *Wire to Wire: Inside the 1984 Detroit Tigers Championship Season* (Chicago: Triumph Books, 2004), p. 134.

IN THE CLUTCH

"All that talk of Cobb...": Cantor, George. *The World Series Fact Book* (Detroit, MI: Visible Ink Press, 1996), p. 26.

"We're either on borrowed time...": Gage, Tom. "Tigers Still Breathing in Toronto," *The Detroit News,* September 28, 1987, section D, p. 1.

"We'd been watching film...": Cantor, George. *The Tigers of '68: Baseball's Last Real Champions* (Dallas, TX: Taylor Publishing, 1997), p. 78.

"I don't think any of us had ever heard of him...": Honig, Donald. *Baseball When the Grass Was Real* (New York: Coward, McCann & Geoghegan, Inc., 1975), p. 272.

"I tried to make everybody think I was calm...": Cantor, George. *The Tigers of '68: Baseball's Last Real Champions* (Dallas, TX: Taylor Publishing, 1997), p. 174.

NUMBERS DON'T LIE (OR DO THEY?)

"He had one of the finest fastballs...": Honig, Donald. *Baseball When the Grass Was Real* (New York: Coward, McCann & Geoghegan, Inc., 1975), p. 47.

"Balls that surely would have been home runs...": Ritter, Lawrence S. *The Glory of Their Times: The Story of the Early Days of Baseball Told by the Men Who Played It* (New York: Macmillan Co., 1966), p. 47

"I'd sort of half glance at Cobb...": ibid., p. 60.

IT AIN'T OVER 'TIL IT'S OVER

"If we had blown the pennant...": Cantor, George. *Wire to Wire: Inside the 1984 Detroit Tigers Championship Season* (Chicago: Triumph Books, 2004), p. 72.

"Darrell Evans had been with the Giants...": ibid., p. 21.

"Hall of Famer Jim Palmer remembered...": Associated Press, Obituary for Steve Barber, February 22, 2007.

"I can't start him and because of his control...": Cantor, George. *The Tigers of '68: Baseball's Last Real Champions* (Dallas, TX: Taylor Publishing, 1997), p. 95.

WHEELIN' AND DEALIN'

"He made Heinie a great hitter...": Honig, Donald. *Baseball When the Grass Was Real* (New York: Coward, McCann & Geoghegan, Inc., 1975), p. 41.

"You didn't beat out Ted Williams too often...": Falls, Joe. *The Detroit Tigers: An Illustrated History* (New York: Walker & Co., 1989), p. 110.

"Never playing in a World Series hurt...": Cantor, George. "The Voice Is Pure Arkansas," *The Detroit News Magazine,* March 7, 1982, p. 10.

A TOUCH OF VIOLENCE

"We had all winter to think about it…": Cantor, George. *The Tigers of '68: Baseball's Last Real Champions* (Dallas, TX: Taylor Publishing, 1997), p. 22.

"I never could figure out where…": Honig, Donald. *Baseball When the Grass Was Real* (New York: Coward, McCann & Geoghegan, Inc., 1975), p. 52.

"The Dizziest, Maddest and Wildest…": Gallico, Paul. "Diz Dazzles," (New York) *Daily News,* October 10, 1934.

JUST PLAIN WEIRD

"Veeck may try this on another day…": Greene, Sam. "New Low in St. Louis," *The Detroit News,* August 20, 1951, section C, p. 1.

TEAMMATES

"Why do they so resent Cobb…": Bak, Richard. *Ty Cobb: His Tumultuous Life and Times* (Dallas, TX: Taylor Publishing, 1994), p. 76.

"The New York broadcasters never saw…": Cantor, George. *The Tigers of '68: Baseball's Last Real Champions* (Dallas, TX: Taylor Publishing, 1997), p. 161.

"People took it for granted…" Cantor, George. *Wire to Wire: Inside the 1984 Detroit Tigers Championship Season* (Chicago: Triumph Books, 2004), p. 138.